Fact Book: The HUGE Book of Amazing Facts and Interesting Stuff

Volume 3: 2020/21

Jenny Kellett

Fact Book: The HUGE Book of Amazing Facts and Interesting Stuff 2020

ISBN: 9798612125211
Independently Published

Facebook: @theworldsbestfacts

www.knowmorestuff.co

Contents

Introduction

Welcome to The HUGE Book of Amazing Facts and Interesting Stuff! We have spent countless hours trawling through incredible, curious facts to bring you only the very best knowledge-boosting titbits.

Since the last version of this book was published, a lot has happened. 2019 was full of crazy politics (Donald Trump, Brexit...) and every other person seemingly turned vegan; then 2020 has started with Meghan Markle and Prince Harry essentially leaving the British Royal family and Australia being ravaged by awful bushfires.

So whether you want to impress your friends or increase your knowledge about the world and our universe, you're in the right place.

Enjoy!

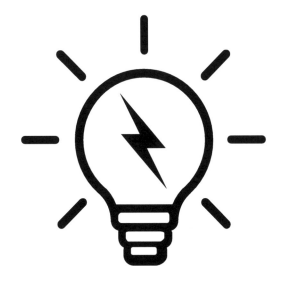

Science & Technology

The world is changing at a rapid pace thanks to advances in science and technology. Who would have thought twenty years ago that we would be carrying phones in our pockets that were smaller and more powerful than a PC? Or that we could have video chats to people on the other side of the world for free via Skype? It's amazing, really.

Enjoy these science & technology facts, and here's to another decade of amazing advancements.

In 2019, a lost continent was found. Greater Adria is located in the Mediterranean region and was discovered by researchers at Utrecht University.

• • •

The food with the highest caloric value is pure animal fat, with nearly 900 calories per 100 grams.

• • •

Every person is only 0.1% different genetically; our closest living relatives — chimpanzees — are 1.2% different from us.

• • •

Approximately 1% of descendants of Northern Europeans have been found to be immune to HIV. Swedes are the least likely to be infected.

There are enormous floating mountains of ice on Pluto.

• • •

The first letter to be sent over the internet was 'L'.

• • •

Water is repelled by a magnet. Try it.

• • •

A study found that if you look at a photo of a loved one, you can reduce pain by around 40%.

• • •

If you could throw a snowball fast enough it would completely vaporize when it hit a brick wall.

Just over two thirds of cancer patients treated in the USA are cured.

• • •

Up until the 1950's, many doctors believed exercise was dangerous for people over the age of 40. They would prescribe bed rest to heart disease sufferers.

• • •

In 2017, scientists found a potential energy source for living beings on Saturn's moon, Enceladus.

• • •

Nomophobia is an addiction to mobile phones. Over 200,000 people suffer from this phobia, which leaves you afraid to leave your home without your mobile phone.

92 per cent of the world's currency exists digitally — the rest is physical money.

• • •

Venus is the only planet in the solar system that spins backwards.

• • •

In 2019, scientists found bones in New Zealand of a human-sized penguin. It is estimated to have lived 60 million years ago.

• • •

In 2019, a Japanese Google employee, Emma Haruka Iwao, calculated Pi to a record 31 trillion digits using the company's cloud computing service.

US astronauts at the International Space Station are sent ballot papers to allow them to vote in elections.

• • •

If you spin a ball as you drop it, it will fly. This is called the Magnus effect.

• • •

In 2017, astronomers could 'hear' space for the first time. It was named the scientific breakthrough of the year by Science magazine.

• • •

Water can boil and freeze at the same time when at certain pressures.

There are more mobile phone connections than people in the world.

• • •

In our galaxy alone there are over 100 billion planets.

• • •

Over three billion people in the world use a mobile phone. Three and a half billion use a toothbrush.

• • •

Popping a cork from a champagne bottle releases the same level of shock waves as a jet.

In the UK, over 86% of breast cancer patients now survive past five years.

• • •

Scientists were able to reverse-engineer chickens to have dinosaur snouts.

• • •

There are flowers that smell like chocolate, including the Chocolate Daisy and the Chocolate Cosmos.

• • •

An owl can hear a mouse more than 50 feet away.

There are over 23,000 pieces of 'space junk' orbiting the Earth, leftover from space missions. In total, these weigh more than 8,000 tons.

• • •

If you crack an egg underwater, it looks like a jellyfish.

• • •

People who can function on only a few hours of sleep a night may have a gene mutation, according to a 2019 study.

• • •

Lasers can get trapped in a waterfall — an example of total internal reflection.

Certain types of beer have the same microbial and probiotic benefits of food products such as sauerkraut, yoghurt and kimchi.

• • •

Before 1995, domain name registrations were free!

• • •

A new beetle discovered by scientists in 2019 was named after Greta Thunberg. The Nelloptodes gretae has antenna that look like braided hair — the most popular style worn by the young activist.

• • •

Sodium in cheese can actually protect your body from cardiovascular disease caused by other salts.

If you squeeze lemon juice on apples and bananas you can prevent oxidation (turning brown).

• • •

A small percentage of the static you see on "dead" TV stations is leftover radiation from the Big Bang.

• • •

Email existed before the World Wide Web.

• • •

There are 20 to 30 times more bacteria on the average mobile phone than what you find in a toilet bowl.

QWERTY keyboards were invented partially to slow down how fast you could type. This was because people were typing too fast and jamming their typewriters.

• • •

The first-ever personal computer was called 'Simon'.

• • •

In 2019, 54.68% of emails sent every day were considered to be spam. This has decreased from 69% in 2012.

• • •

If you use a lighter style font when printing, you can save up to 10% ink so your printer cartridges will last longer!

In 1956, 5 MB of data literally weighed a ton, and required a forklift to move it.

• • •

Over 90% of text messages sent are read within three minutes of being delivered, and 99% are ever read.

• • •

In 2019, engineers proved that Leonardo Da Vinci's designs for the world's largest bridge at the time would have worked. It was intended to connect Istanbul with the neighbouring city of Galata.

Mars is covered in rust, which is why it appears red.

• • •

Osmium and iridium are the densest metals in the world, while plutonium and uranium are the heaviest metals based on relative atomic mass.

• • •

One in three deaths around the world is caused by cardiovascular disease.

• • •

The dots in Gmail addresses are redundant. For example, if your email address is joeblogs@gmail.com, someone could email joe.blogs.@gmail.com and it would still get to you.

Human bodies are able to move for more than a year after death. Don't be alarmed though, this is caused by the body's ligaments shrinking, drying out and contracting.

• • •

700 million years ago, Venus may have been hospitable.

• • •

When you move your eyes, your eardrums also move.

• • •

Two 700-year old skeletons that were found in the Italian city of Modena holding each others hands in 2009 and nicknamed the 'Lovers of Modena', were found to be both male by scientists in 2019.

Some studies have shown that intelligent people have more copper and zinc in their hair.

• • •

A 'jiffy' is an actual unit of time. It has been redefined over the years, but was originally defined as the time it takes for light to travel one centimeter in a vacuum.

• • •

Time slows down near black holes. Inside of it, it completely stops.

• • •

When lightning strikes a sandy beach that is high in silica or quartz, it produces glass.

A hurricane can produce as much energy as 10,000 nuclear bombs during its life cycle.

• • •

On average, humans remember 5,000 different faces.

• • •

It's impossible to burp in space.

• • •

Komodo dragons have a suit of armour made of tiny bones underneath their already scaly skin.

• • •

Goats are able to snack on poison ivy with no issues.

In zero gravity conditions, a candle's flame is blue and round, because fire behaves differently in space.

• • •

There are more lifeforms living on your skin than people on the planet. In fact, most of the time we have over 90 trillion microbes living on us.

• • •

The US has blown up multiple atomic and hydrogen bombs in space. The most famous was in 1962, 250 miles above the Pacific Ocean. There is some spectacular video footage if you search online.

• • •

Strawberries are the only fruit that have their seeds on the outside.

A single bat can consume up to 1,000 mosquitoes in an hour.

• • •

Penguins and ostriches are the only birds that can swim, but not fly.

• • •

Two million blood cells die every second. But don't be alarmed, two million blood cells are also created every second.

• • •

It takes about 37 gallons of water to produce a single cup of coffee.

You can clean your toilet using Gatorade. Simply pour two cups of the drink into the toilet and leave for one hour, then brush away.

• • •

Hot water freezes faster than cold water. This is called the Mbemba effect.

• • •

The Dvorak keyboard is 74% faster to type on that the QWERTY keyboard, once you have completed training.

• • •

There are more nerve connectors in your brain than there are stars in the galaxy. A piece of brain tissue the size of a grain of sand contains over 100,000 neurons.

Diamonds can grow inside other diamonds. The first example was found in 2019.

• • •

Dolphins are right-handed.

• • •

Shaking your head after getting water in your ears may cause brain damage.

• • •

If you put grapes in the microwave they will explode.

• • •

Giraffes who have dark spots are more dominant than those with light spots.

An ear of corn always has an even number of rows (usually from 8 to 22).

• • •

Everyone has a unique tongue print, just like a fingerprint.

• • •

There is a disease called Alien Hand Syndrome (AHS), in which the person has no conscious control over his 'alien hand' and will blurt things out like: "I swear I'm not doing this". It is also known as Dr Strangelove Syndrome.

• • •

There are more drops of water in the ocean than there are atoms in a drop of water, but only just!

The Bee Gees' song Stayin' Alive is used to train medical professionals to provide the correct number of chest compressions per minute while performing CPR.

• • •

Just 100 nanograms of botulinum toxin — the most deadly toxin in the world — could kill a human being. Just 1kg could wipe out the entire human race. However, people willfully use it in the form of Botox to freeze muscles in their face.

• • •

Every hour, there are around 760 thunderstorms on Earth.

The hardest working muscles in the human body are in the eyes. In one hour of reading, the eye makes nearly 10,000 movements.

• • •

The state of California supplies over 80% of the USA's broccoli.

• • •

If you removed all the empty space inside of humans, the entire human race would fit into the volume of a sugar cube. This is because we are 99.9999999999% empty matter.

• • •

By 2050 there will be more plastic in the oceans than there are fish (by weight).

If you take part in physical exercise four hours after learning something, it has been shown to help improve your long-term memory.

• • •

Feet have the highest concentration of sweat glands of any part of the body, and can produce more than a pint of sweat a day.

• • •

When you see most stars, you're essentially looking perhaps hundreds or thousands of years into the past, as that's how long the light takes to reach us.

Rabies has a fatality rate of almost 100%.

• • •

There is a mathematical theorem called 'Hairy Balls Theorem'. The theorem states colloquially that: "you can't comb a hairy ball flat without creating a cowlick".

• • •

It takes 17 muscles to smile and 43 to frown (although this varies on the size of the smile/frown and the individual's face, of course). So, smile more!

• • •

If you cut up a hologram, the entire image is retained in each piece.

The Pratfall Effect is a psychological phenomenon whereby a person who is deemed attractive or competent by someone is found to be even more so if they commit a blunder, such as tripping over.

• • •

People don't actually get sick from cold weather; they get sick because viruses thrive better in cooler air. Also, we spend more time indoors when it's cold, and are in closer contact with infected people.

• • •

Girls are generally better at recognising different tastes than boys.

• • •

Some spiders are able to make milk for their babies.

A study found that hard-to-read handwriting is actually more convincing, as the reader has to read slower and consider the argument more carefully.

• • •

Men who look up to superheroes often have a more positive body image.

• • •

A set of human lungs has a surface area around 180 m2, similar to that of a tennis court.

• • •

The largest snowflake ever recorded measured 15 inches across. It was discovered by a ranch owner in Montana in 1887.

The average human body contains enough fat to make seven bars of soap.

• • •

Dirty snow melts faster than clean snow, because the dark colour absorbs more energy from the sun.

• • •

Since being discovered in 1930, Pluto has not yet completed a full orbit of the Sun. One Plutonian year is 247.68 Earth years.

• • •

Babies start dreaming before they are born.

Scientists at Columbia University have been able to grow heart muscle from human stem cells.

• • •

Men are more likely to develop long-term hiccups than women.

• • •

When glass breaks, the cracks move at speeds of up to 3,000 miles per hour.

• • •

In one acre of land, there can be more than one million earthworms.

A zebra is black with white stripes.

• • •

When baby sharks are born, they swim away from their mothers and live on their own immediately.

• • •

It can take a photon 40,000 years to travel from the core of the sun to the surface, but only 8 minutes to travel the rest of the way to earth.

• • •

In 1936, Russia built an analog computer that ran on water called the Water Integrator. It could solve partial differential equations.

Honey contains hydrogen peroxide, which makes it a great natural antiseptic.

• • •

It is impossible to kill yourself by holding your breath.

• • •

The first computer programmers were women. Ada Lovelace was the first person to publish an algorithm to be executed by the world's first modern computer.

• • •

Icebergs can weigh more than 10 million tonnes.

Peanuts are legumes and are not tree nuts.

• • •

There is around $771 trillion worth of gold floating in the oceans — but it's in such small pieces that it would be almost impossible to harvest.

• • •

The longest time that has gone between two twins being born was 87 days. They were born in Ireland in 2012.

• • •

There's enough water pressure in one onion cell to cause a steam engine to explode.

Sources

1. *There's a Lost Continent Hiding Beneath Europe.* https://www.livescience.com/ancient-lost-continent-beneath-europe.html
2. *Calories in 100 g of Animal Fat or Drippings and Nutrition Facts* https://www.fatsecret.com/calories-nutrition/generic/animal-fat-or-drippings
3. https://www.nasa.gov/mission_pages/kepler/news/kepler20130103.html#.UrIUHmRDt-WZ
4. *Far from special: Humanity's tiny DNA differences are 'average' in animal kingdom* https://phys.org/news/2018-05-special-humanity-tiny-dna-differences.html
5. *Genetic HIV Resistance Deciphered* https://www.wired.com/2005/01/genetic-hiv-resistance-deciphered/
6. *The First Characters Sent Through the Internet Were L-O-L* https://www.theatlantic.com/technology/archive/2014/10/the-first-characters-sent-through-the-internet-were-l-o-l/382074/
7. *How many faces do people know? | Proceedings of the Royal Society B: Biological Sciences* https://royalsocietypublishing.org/doi/full/10.1098/rspb.2018.1319
8. *Venus Could Have Been Habitable for Billions of Years* https://www.smithsonianmag.com/smart-news/venus-could-have-been-habitable-billions-years-180973203/
9. *The eardrums move when the eyes move: A multisensory effect on the mechanics of hearing* https://www.pnas.org/content/115/6/E1309
10. *Potential Energy Source for Life Spotted on Saturn Moon Enceladus* https://www.space.com/36455-saturn-moon-enceladus-energy-source-life.html
11. https://vis.sciencemag.org/breakthrough2017/finalists/#cosmic-convergence
12. *Do Magnets Work Under Water?* https://terpconnect.umd.edu/~wbreslyn/magnets/do-magnets-work-under-water.html
13. *Love Can Relieve Pain* https://well.blogs.nytimes.com/2010/10/13/love-and-pain-relief/
14. *View More Fun Facts* https://www.mcwane.org/fun-facts/
15. *20 out of last 22 years warmest on record* https://www.deccanherald.com/national/20-out-last-22-years-warmest-706147.html
16. *12 mobile phone facts that will shock you, keep reading to find out* https://ehorus.com/mobile-phone-facts/
17. *Cancer Treatment at the End of Life* https://www.nytimes.com/2019/08/05/well/live/cancer-treatment-at-the-end-of-life.html

18. *How Many Steps Should You Take a Day?* https://www.nytimes.com/2019/08/21/magazine/how-many-steps-should-you-take-a-day.html

19. *FlashReport Disfluency disrupts the confirmation bias* https://www.sciencedirect.com/science/article/abs/pii/S002210311200176X

20. *Prolonged milk provisioning in a jumping spider* https://science.sciencemag.org/content/362/6418/1052

21. *Batman to the rescue! The protective effects of parasocial relationships with muscular superheroes on men's body image* https://www.sciencedirect.com/science/article/abs/pii/S0022103112001552

22. *5 Amazing Things We've Learned a Year After Visiting Pluto* https://www.nationalgeographic.com/news/2016/07/pluto-planets-new-horizons-one-year-anniversary-nasa-space-science/

23. *92% of The world's currency is digital* https://timesofindia.indiatimes.com/12-weird-but-true-facts-about-technology/92-of-the-worlds-currency-is-digital/photostory/51422304.cms

24. *Why Venus Spins the Wrong Way* https://www.scientificamerican.com/article/why-venus-spins-the-wrong/

25. *Emma Haruka Iwao smashes pi world record with Google help* https://www.bbc.com/news/technology-47524760

26. *Astronaut Casts Election Day Vote from International Space Station* https://www.forbes.com/sites/lisettevoytko/2019/11/05/astronaut-casts-election-day-vote-from-international-space-station/#5bd051a915d6

27. *Magnus effect | physics | Britannica* https://www.britannica.com/science/Magnus-effect

28. *'Human-sized penguin' lived in New Zealand* https://www.bbc.com/news/world-asia-49340715

29. *Watch a Liquid Boil And Freeze at The Same Time* https://www.sciencealert.com/watch-a-liquid-boil-and-freeze-at-the-same-time

30. *How Many People Have Smartphones Worldwide (Jan 2020)* https://www.bankmycell.com/blog/how-many-phones-are-in-the-world

31. https://www.cancerresearchuk.org/health-professional/cancer-statistics/statistics-by-cancer-type/breast-cancer/survival#heading-Zero

32. *Best Chocolate Scented Flowers | Plants That Smell Like Chocolate* https://balconygardenweb.com/best-chocolate-scented-flowers-plants-and-flowers-that-smell-like-flower/

33. *Under-expanded supersonic CO_2 freezing jets during champagne cork popping* https://advances.sciencemag.org/content/5/9/eaav5528.full

34. *The Great Horned Owl* http://owls.wpstudent.net/hoots/who/great-horned-owl/

35. *Will space be kept clean of debris? Americans are skeptical* https://www.pewresearch.org/fact-tank/2018/08/31/as-debris-piles-up-americans-are-skeptical-enough-will-be-done-to-limit-space-junk/

36. *What Happens When You Crack An Egg Underwater?* https://www.youtube.com/watch?v=rJmoROaMduQ

37. *Can laser get trapped in a waterfall?* https://telanganatoday.com/laser-trapped-waterfall

38. *Domain Names History* https://mashable.com/2014/03/10/domain-names-history

39. *Lemon Juice on Apples Experiment* https://learning-center.homesciencetools.com/article/acid-keeps-apple-fresh/

40. *20 fascinating facts that will make you think twice* https://www.independent.co.uk/news/weird-news/20-fascinating-facts-that-will-make-you-think-twice-a6747011.html

41. *A Rare Mutation of β1-Adrenergic Receptor Affects Sleep/Wake Behaviors* https://www.cell.com/neuron/fulltext/S0896-6273(19)30652-X

42. *Scientists praise stronger beers as 'very, very healthy' thanks to gut-friendly bacteria* https://www.independent.co.uk/life-style/food-and-drink/beer-healthy-probiotic-belgian-beers-hoegaarden-westmalle-eric-claasen-gut-a9227106.html

43. *Michael Darby* https://nhm.academia.edu/MichaelDarby

44. *Controlled Feeding of an 8-d, High-Dairy Cheese Diet Prevents Sodium-Induced Endothelial Dysfunction in the Cutaneous Microcirculation of Healthy, Older Adults through Reductions in Superoxide* https://academic.oup.com/jn/advance-article-abstract/doi/10.1093/jn/nxz205/5556064?redirectedFrom=fulltext

45. *Cast-iron cookware* https://en.wikipedia.org/wiki/Cast-iron_cookware

46. *The history of email* http://www.nethistory.info/History%20of%20the%20Internet/email.html

47. *Email existed before the world wide web - 12 weird but true facts about technology* https://economictimes.indiatimes.com/tech-life/12-weird-but-true-facts-about-technology/email-existed-before-the-world-wide-web/slideshow/51419395.cms

48. *Simon* http://www.historyofinformation.com/detail.php?entryid=95

49. *Spam statistics: spam e-mail traffic share 2019* https://www.statista.com/statistics/420391/spam-email-traffic-share/

50. *10 Tips to Save on Ink When Printing | HP® Tech Takes* https://store.hp.com/us/en/tech-takes/10-tips-save-on-ink-when-printing

51. *What a 5MB Hard Drive Looked Like in 1956* https://thenextweb.com/shareables/2011/12/26/this-is-what-a-5mb-hard-drive-looked-like-is-1956-required-a-forklift/

52. *Engineers put Leonardo da Vinci's bridge design to the test* http://news.mit.edu/2019/leonardo-da-vinci-bridge-test-1010

53. *Conversational Advertising* https://mobilesquared.co.uk/wp-content/uploads/2017/12/Conversational-Advertising.pdf

54. *Why is Mars red?* https://www.childrensmuseum.org/blog/why-mars-red

55. *Which Metals Are the Heaviest?* https://sciencing.com/metals-heaviest-8751708.html

56. *Cardiovascular disease causes one-third of deaths worldwide: 'Alarming trends' for countries in all stages of development* https://www.sciencedaily.com/releases/2017/05/170517143625.htm

57. *Dots don't matter in Gmail addresses - Gmail Help* https://support.google.com/mail/answer/7436150?hl=en

58. *Jiffy (time)* https://en.wikipedia.org/wiki/Jiffy_(time)

59. *Dead bodies move while decomposing, a significant find for death investigations* https://www.abc.net.au/news/2019-09-12/dead-bodies-move-while-decomposing-significant-find-for-police/11492330

60. *Gli "amanti di Modena" erano due individui di sesso maschile* https://magazine.unibo.it/archivio/2019/09/11/gli-201camanti-di-modena201d-erano-due-individui-di-sesso-maschile

61. *The Cephalic Osteoderms of Varanus komodoensis as Revealed by High‑Resolution XRay Computed Tomography* https://anatomypubs.onlinelibrary.wiley.com/doi/10.1002/ar.24197

62. http://eng.alrosa.ru/58808/

63. *Behavioural laterality in foraging bottlenose dolphins (Tursiops truncatus) | Royal Society Open Science* https://royalsocietypublishing.org/doi/10.1098/rsos.190929

64. *72nd Annual Meeting of the APS Division of Fluid Dynamics - Event - Acceleration-induced water ejection in the human ear canal* http://meetings.aps.org/Meeting/DFD19/Session/A31.7

65. *Relationships between male giraffes' colour, age and sociability* https://www.sciencedirect.com/science/article/pii/S0003347219302453?via%3Dihub

66. *Linking plasma formation in grapes to microwave resonances of aqueous dimers* https://www.pnas.org/content/116/10/4000

67. *Do Intelligent People Have More Zinc and Copper in their Hair?* http://www.didyouknow.it/people/intelligent-people-have-more-zinc-and-copper-in-their-hair/

68. *Universe Forum--Black Holes--What are they?* https://www.cfa.harvard.edu/seuforum/bh_whatare.htm

69. *What Really Happens When Lightning Strikes Sand: The Science Behind a Viral Photo* https://www.discovermagazine.com/the-sciences/what-really-happens-when-lightning-strikes-sand-the-science-behind-a-viral-photo

70. *How much energy in a hurricane, a volcano, and an earthquake?* https://science.howstuffworks.com/environmental/energy/energy-hurricane-volcano-earthquake1.htm

71. *Can you burp in space?* https://qz.com/1449587/can-you-burp-in-space/

72. *In zero gravity, a candle's flame is round and blue!* https://saveourgreen.org/allpost/in-zero-gravity-a-candles-flame-is-round-and-blue/

73. *Your body is a planet* https://www.discovermagazine.com/health/your-body-is-a-planet

74. *Go Ahead Little Goat Eat Some Poison Ivy* https://www.npr.org/sections/goatsand-soda/2015/04/06/397879410/go-ahead-little-goat-eat-some-poison-ivy-it-wont-hurt-a-bit

75. *A Very Scary Light Show: Exploding H-Bombs In Space* https://www.npr.org/sections/krulwich/2010/07/01/128170775/a-very-scary-light-show-exploding-h-bombs-in-space

76. *14 Things You Didn't Know About Strawberries* https://www.foodrepublic.com/2013/05/20/14-things-you-didnt-know-about-strawberries/

77. *Learn Some Amazing Bat Facts* http://www.batrescue.org/batfacts/batfacts.html

78. *8 Birds That Can't Fly* https://www.britannica.com/list/8-birds-that-cant-fly

79. *UCSB Science Line* http://scienceline.ucsb.edu/getkey.php?key=4831

80. *The New Plastics Economy: Rethinking the future of plastics & catalysing action* https://www.ellenmacarthurfoundation.org/publications/the-new-plastics-economy-rethinking-the-future-of-plastics-catalysing-action

81. *The water footprint of your coffee* https://coffeelands.crs.org/2012/09/302-the-water-footprint-of-your-coffee/

82. *Clean A Toilet Bowl With Gatorade* https://www.huffpost.com/entry/clean-a-toilet-bowl-gatorade_n_2451993

83. *Why Hot Water Freezes Faster Than Cold—Physicists Solve the Mpemba Effect* https://medium.com/the-physics-arxiv-blog/why-hot-water-freezes-faster-than-cold-physicists-solve-the-mpemba-effect-d8a2f611e853

84. *Dvorak* http://www.mit.edu/~jcb/Dvorak/

85. *Why Your Brain is Like The Universe | BrainMD Life* https://brainmd.com/blog/how-your-brain-is-like-the-universe/#

86. *It's Corny, But It's REALLY Yummy* https://wzozfm.com/its-corny-but-its-really-yummy/

87. *Tongue Print - 16 Unusual Facts About the Human Body | HowStuffWorks* https://health.howstuffworks.com/human-body/parts/16-unusual-facts-about-the-human-body1.htm

88. *Can The Entire Human Race Fit Inside A Sugar Cube?* https://www.scienceabc.com/pure-sciences/can-the-entire-human-race-fit-inside-a-sugar-cube.html

89. *Alien hand syndrome* https://en.wikipedia.org/wiki/Alien_hand_syndrome

90. *Bee Gees song Stayin' Alive helps doctors perform CPR* https://www.telegraph.co.uk/news/worldnews/northamerica/usa/3214030/Bee-Gees-song-Stayin-Alive-helps-

43

doctors-perform-CPR.html

91. *The drugs derived from deadly poisons* https://www.bbc.com/news/magazine-24551945

92. *Thunderstorm numbers calculated* https://www.bbc.com/news/science-environment-12991483

93. *What is the strongest muscle in the human body?* https://www.loc.gov/everyday-mysteries/item/what-is-the-strongest-muscle-in-the-human-body/

94. *How Many Molecules Are in a Drop of Water?* https://www.thoughtco.com/atoms-in-a-drop-of-water-609425

95. *U.S.-Mexico Fruit and Vegetable Trade*, 1970-92 — Susan L. Pollack

96. *Physical Exercise Performed Four Hours after Learning Improves Memory Retention and Increases Hippocampal Pattern Similarity during Retrieval*. https://www.ncbi.nlm.nih.gov/pubmed/27321998

97. *Sweaty Feet | Why do my feet sweat? | Treatment* https://patient.info/skin-conditions/excessive-sweating-hyperhidrosis/sweaty-feet

98. *How can the Hubble Space Telescope look back in time?* https://spaceplace.nasa.gov/review/dr-marc-technology/hubble.html

99. *Hairy ball theorem* https://en.wikipedia.org/wiki/Hairy_ball_theorem

100. *A Presumptive Case of Human Rabies: A Rare Survived Case in Rural Ghana* https://www.ncbi.nlm.nih.gov/pmc/articles/PMC5104963/

101. *How many muscles does it take to smile?* https://science.howstuffworks.com/life/inside-the-mind/emotions/muscles-smile.htm

102. *How Holograms Work* https://science.howstuffworks.com/hologram.htm

103. *Pratfall effect* https://en.wikipedia.org/wiki/Pratfall_effect

104. *What's the Link Between Cold Weather and the Common Cold?* https://www.medicalnewstoday.com/articles/323431.php#cold-weather-and-viruses

105. *Girls Have Superior Sense Of Taste To Boys* https://www.sciencedaily.com/releases/2008/12/081216104035.htm

106. *The surface area of a pair of lungs is equal to that of a tennis court* https://vedanadosah.cvtisr.sk/en/the-surface-area-of-a-pair-of-lungs-is-equal-to-that-of-a-tennis-court

107. *How Big Can Snowflakes Be?* https://news.ncsu.edu/2018/12/how-big-can-snowflakes-be/

108. *Wednesday Wisdom: Your Body Has Enough of this to Produce Over 7 Bars of Soap?* https://www.somatechnology.com/blog/wednesday-wisdom/wednesday-wisdom-your-body-has-enough-of-this-to-produce-over-7-bars-of-soap/

109. *Dusting the Virtues of Snow* https://earthobservatory.nasa.gov/features/DirtySnow

110. *Pluto* https://en.wikipedia.org/wiki/Pluto

111. *What do Babies Dream about in the Womb?* https://www.eqdiapers.com.ph/good_

reads/what-do-babies-dream-about-in-the-womb

112. *Human Heart Muscle Stem Cells* https://engineering.columbia.edu/news/human-heart-muscle-stem-cells

113. *AP Physics B Handbook* - Hasan Fakhruddin

114. *Worm Facts | The Adventures of Herman the Worm* https://web.extension.illinois.edu/worms/facts/

115. *Zebra* https://en.wikipedia.org/wiki/Zebra

116. *Facts About Great White Sharks* https://www.livescience.com/27338-great-white-sharks.html

117. *A Sunshine Holiday (How the Sun Works)* https://futurism.com/how-the-sun-works

118. *Water integrator* https://en.wikipedia.org/wiki/Water_integrator

119. *How honey heals wounds* https://www.sciencelearn.org.nz/resources/1702-how-honey-heals-wounds

120. *Why Can't You Hold Your Breath Until You're Dead? | Evolutionary Psychology Blog Archive* http://web.sas.upenn.edu/kurzbanepblog/2011/02/07/why-cant-you-hold-your-breath-until-youre-dead/

121. *Women in computing* https://en.wikipedia.org/wiki/Women_in_computing

122. *Newfoundland and Labrador Iceberg Facts* https://www.newfoundlandlabrador.com/trip-ideas/travel-stories/iceberg-facts

123. *Peanut vs. Tree Nuts Allergy and Why It Matters — IFIC Foundation* https://foodinsight.org/peanut-vs-tree-nuts-allergy-and-why-it-matters/

124. *771 Trillion Worth of Gold Hidden in the Ocean* https://www.forbes.com/sites/trevornace/2017/09/15/771-trillion-worth-gold-hidden-ocean/#6f9d388923d3

125. *Longest interval between birth of twins* https://www.guinnessworldrecords.com/world-records/67465-longest-interval-between-birth-of-twins/

126. *Steam Engine* http://www.finedictionary.com/steam%20engine.html

127. *Hiccups* https://www.mayoclinic.org/diseases-conditions/hiccups/symptoms-causes/syc-20352613

Animals & Nature

Just step outside and look around you — it's incredible, really! On our planet there are millions of species of plants and animals, all of which have their own unique characteristics and amazing tricks. And let's not get started on our planet itself... we're spinning in space?! Incredible.

A lamb can identify its mother by her bleating sound.

• • •

Spiders have transparent blood. The colourless blood is called hemolymph.

• • •

It takes 1,000 years for the average piece of plastic to break down. Even then, it will just break down into smaller pieces of plastic.

• • •

Cats were never mentioned in the Bible.

It is believed that dinosaurs may have shed their skin in chunks, rather than all at once like modern reptiles.

• • •

Cats are able to recognise their own names, but they also have the ability to choose to ignore it when they choose to.

• • •

A tiny breed of shark was discovered in 2015 (but only recognised as a new species in 2019). It is only 5.5 cm in length and looks like a miniature sperm whale.

Ducks can see ultraviolet light.

• • •

There is a type of psychoactive fungus that can make cicadas butts fall off when they come into contact with it.

• • •

Only female mosquitoes bite, because they need protein from blood to help the eggs develop.

• • •

Carrots used to be purple, yellow and white — but not orange.

The weight of a cow can vary by 75 lb in one day.

• • •

In 2017 and 2019, green coloured puppies were born. However, this was due to bile pigment in the womb and it eventually faded.

• • •

Nearly 10 horses die every week on American race tracks, more than any other country in the world.

• • •

Bed bugs were around at the same time as the dinosaurs, but they survived the extinction.

The brains of some tiny spiders overflow into their legs.

• • •

Female kangaroos have three vaginas.

• • •

In one season, a single seahorse can produce over 2,000 babies. And it's the males that give birth, not the females.

• • •

Flamingos get their pink color from their food. They eat tiny blue-green algae and shrimp that turn pink during digestion.

Jellyfish evaporate in the sun. They are 98% water.

• • •

A full bladder is about the size of a soft ball.

• • •

A small blue fruit that grows in parts of Africa is the world's most intense natural colour.

• • •

More than 90% of greenhouse gases being trapped by the Earth are stored in the oceans.

• • •

Octopuses have three hearts.

During solar eclipses, bees stop buzzing.

• • •

Human birth control pills work on gorillas.

• • •

In a study, pigeons were able to learn all the letters of the alphabet.

• • •

Tigers have striped skin.

• • •

The Mimosa Pudica, an exotic herb from South and Central America is able to learn and remember things as well as many animals.

Elephants have their own alarm call, which means 'humans'.

• • •

There are approximately 8.7 million species of animals and 391,000 species of plants on Earth.

• • •

Azara's owl monkeys are more monogamous than humans.

• • •

The legs of a Tyrannosaurus Rex were about 12 feet long. It's arms were only 3 feet long, in comparison.

Castoreum is an anal secretion that beavers use to mark their territories. It smells like vanilla and is actually used in food and perfume, and is often labeled as natural flavouring.

• • •

The reason our fingers get wrinkly when left in water is the body's way of helping us have a better grip on objects that are wet.

• • •

Babies are born without kneecaps. Kneecaps develop around the age of four.

• • •

Reindeer eyeballs turn blue in winter to help them see at lower light levels.

Owls don't have eyeballs. They have eye tubes.

• • •

Sloths can hold their breath underwater for 40 minutes.

• • •

Mosquitoes are attracted to the color blue twice as much as any other color.

• • •

Giraffes have one of the highest blood pressures of all animals, due to the distance between their head and heart.

Wombat poop is in the shape of a cube.

• • •

If an octopus is scared or angry, it can turn a different color.

• • •

Teeth start growing about six months before you're born, they're just not visible for around 6-12 months.

• • •

Apples can wake you up better than coffee, as they contain 13g of natural sugar.

The 20 warmest years ever on record have all been in the last 22 years.

• • •

Some catfish are able to kill pigeons.

• • •

If all the land glaciers in the world were to melt, the water they would release could raise ocean levels by more than 70m.

• • •

Moths can't fly during an earthquake.

• • •

A fetus in the womb can get hiccups.

You are taller in the morning — the cartilage between your bones compresses throughout the day, meaning you can be up to 1 cm shorter at the end of the day.

• • •

On a pound-for-pound basis, human babies are stronger than oxen.

• • •

Clown fish start off as males and develop into females later on in life.

• • •

Kittens sleep so much because a growth hormone is released only while they are sleeping.

Recycling a three-foot stack of newspapers can save a whole tree.

• • •

Butterflies need to have a body temperature of less than 82 degrees to be able to fly.

• • •

House flies have a lifespan of around two weeks up to a month.

• • •

When a male donkey and a female horse mate, the offspring are called mules. However, when a male horse and female donkey mate, the offspring are called hinnies.

Cats will almost never meow at another cat. Cats use this sound for humans.

• • •

Dogs are able to learn words. A Border Collie named Rico learnt 200 different objects by name.

• • •

It would take 1,200,000 mosquitoes, each sucking once, to completely drain the average human of blood.

• • •

You're more likely to be killed by a dog or a cow than a shark.

Rhino horns are worth about $9,000 per pound in Asia, which is what fuels the poaching trade in Africa.

• • •

When the moon is directly over your head you weigh slightly less.

• • •

The world's most common disease is tooth decay.

• • •

The clownfish is able to change its sex.

Apes suffer from midlife crises just like humans do.

• • •

Your skin is your largest organ.

• • •

A mantis shrimp can swing its claw so fast it boils the water around it and creates a flash of light.

• • •

To know when to mate, a male giraffe will continuously headbutt the female in the bladder until she urinates. The male then tastes the urine and that helps it determine whether the female is ovulating.

Elephants can be pregnant for up to two years.

• • •

Honey is the only food that doesn't spoil.

• • •

Alpacas can get sick or die from loneliness, so it is always best to keep them in pairs, or bigger groups.

• • •

In South Africa, new technology was used to reduce animal poaching by 96% in one national park. They hope to use this technology across the country.

Kangaroos use their tails as a third leg. This is called the 'tripod stance'.

• • •

You can see Australia's Great Barrier Reef from space.

• • •

A hummingbird visits an average of 1,000 flowers a day for nectar.

• • •

The blood of mammals is red; the blood of insects is yellow, and the blood of lobsters is blue (it is clear, but turns blue in contact with oxygen).

The nail of your middle finger grows the fastest, and your thumb nail grows the slowest.

• • •

If you plant an apple seed it is almost guaranteed to grow a tree of a different type of apple.

• • •

A study found that pigs are on the same intellectual level as chimpanzees.

• • •

A group of frogs is called an army.

Two-thirds of the world's polar bears live in Canada.

• • •

Camels can drink 53 gallons of water in just three minutes.

• • •

Camel milk does not curdle.

• • •

Tigers might be known as great hunters, but in fact, only 10% of their hunts end successfully.

• • •

Outbreaks of the bubonic plague (the Black Death) still occur around the world today.

A hummingbird weighs less than a penny.

• • •

A dolphin's blowhole is an evolved nose that is positioned at the top of the dolphin's head.

• • •

The saliva of a chameleon is 400 times thicker than human saliva.

• • •

Cast iron cookware can leach iron into our food, making it great for anemics.

A 49 million year old cockroach fossil was found in 2014.

• • •

Owls cannot move their eyeballs.

• • •

Dogs and humans are the only animals with prostates.

• • •

Male turkeys are called gobblers.

• • •

There are over 2,000 species of starfish worldwide.

Birds fly in a 'v' formation to save energy.

• • •

Female glow-worms use their luminous tails to attract mates.

• • •

As they turn into moths, caterpillars almost completely liquify.

• • •

The tongue of a blue whale can weigh as much as an elephant.

A 15-year-old cat has probably spent about 10 years of its life sleeping.

• • •

Bees have five eyes.

• • •

In the winter, camels can survive six or seven months without drinking any water.

• • •

If a lobster loses an appendage, it can grow another one.

• • •

The urine of a Maned Wolf smells like marijuana.

More than four million hectares of forest are lost every year in Africa.

• • •

The human brain is about 73% water.

• • •

During the last ice age, beavers that were eight feet long roamed the Earth.

• • •

Bamboo can grow up to 36 inches in a single day.

• • •

Dogs watch more television now than a few years ago because modern televisions flicker at a speed that dogs are now able to process.

A Russian man grew a two-inch fir tree in his lung. He thought it was a cancerous tumour, but surgeons found the tree when operating.

• • •

Stingrays are able to jump out of the water.

• • •

Horned toads can shoot blood from their eyeballs.

• • •

Every night, we sleep with up to 10 million mites in the bed.

Sources

1. *How and when do lambs recognize the bleats of their mothers?* http://www.bio-acoustics.info/article/how-and-when-do-lambs-recognize-bleats-their-mothers

2. *The spider blood circulation* https://ednieuw.home.xs4all.nl/Spiders/InfoNed/blood.html

3. *The Truth About Plastic — TekPak Solutions* https://steve-reble-dzwb.squarespace.com/the-truth-about-biodegradable-plastic

4. *List of animals in the Bible* https://en.wikipedia.org/wiki/List_of_animals_in_the_Bible

5. *Why do only female mosquitoes bite? - Revista Mètode* https://metode.org/metodes-whys-and-wherefores/why-do-only-female-mosquitoes-bite.html

6. *Adorable Shark Fits in Your Hand, Looks Like a Mini Sperm Whale* https://www.livescience.com/65989-american-pocket-shark-new-species.html

7. *Discovery of psychoactive plant and mushroom alkaloids in ancient fungal cicada pathogens* https://www.biorxiv.org/content/10.1101/375105v1

8. *Mimosa Plants Have Long Term Memory, Can Learn, Biologists Say | Biology* http://www.sci-news.com/biology/science-mimosa-plants-memory-01695.html

9. *This African Fruit Produces the World's Most Intense Natural Color* https://www.smithsonianmag.com/science-nature/this-african-fruit-produces-the-worlds-most-intense-natural-color-30070457/

10. *Robotic Milkers and an Automated Greenhouse: Inside a High-Tech Small Farm* https://www.nytimes.com/2019/01/13/technology/farm-technology-milkers-robots.html

11. *A Bird's-Eye View* https://www.ducks.org/conservation/waterfowl-research-science/a-birds-eye-view

12. *Domestic cats (Felis catus) discriminate their names from other words* https://www.nature.com/articles/s41598-019-40616-4

13. *Dinosaur dandruff reveals first evidence of skin shedding* https://www.bbc.com/news/science-environment-44252455

14. *Golden Retriever Gives Birth To A Green Puppy Named 'Mojito'* https://www.iflscience.com/plants-and-animals/golden-retriever-gives-birth-to-a-green-puppy-named-mojito/

15. *Horse racing's uncomfortable truth: Horses die — 87 last year alone in Pa.* https://www.pennlive.com/news/2019/05/horse-racings-uncomfortable-truth-horses-die-at-a-rate-of-more-than-one-per-week-in-pa.html

16. *Bedbugs survived the dinosaur extinction event* https://www.bbc.com/news/science-environment-48274090

17. *Rico (dog)* https://en.wikipedia.org/wiki/Rico_(dog)

18. *Rhino Poacher Killed by Elephant and Eaten by Lions, Officials Say* https://www.nytimes.com/2019/04/07/world/africa/south-africa-poacher-rhino-lions.html

19. *The catfish that strands itself to kill pigeons* https://www.discovermagazine.com/planet-earth/the-catfish-that-strands-itself-to-kill-pigeons#.Xcnlu5NKiqD

20. *Bringing Back Dinosaurs — Jurassic World Dinosaur Evolution* https://www.popularmechanics.com/science/animals/a21622026/jurassic-world-how-to-clone-a-dinosaur/

21. *Oceana Study Reveals Seafood Fraud Nationwide* http://oceana.org/sites/default/files/National_Seafood_Fraud_Testing_Results_Highlights_FINAL.pdf

22. *Busy Bees Take a Break During Total Solar Eclipses* https://www.smithsonianmag.com/science-nature/busy-bees-take-break-during-total-solar-eclipses-180970502/

23. *Tiny Tyrannosaur Hints at How T. Rex Became King* https://www.nytimes.com/2019/02/21/science/tiny-tyrannosaur-fossil.html

24. *Why carrots are orange (and 5 non-orange carrots to grow in your garden)* https://www.treehugger.com/lawn-garden/why-carrots-are-orange-and-5-non-orange-carrots-grow-your-garden.html

25. *Tiny Spider Brains Overflow Into The Body, Legs* https://scitechdaily.com/tiny-spider-brains-overflow-into-the-body-legs/

26. *Kangaroos have three vaginas* https://www.discovermagazine.com/the-sciences/kangaroos-have-three-vaginas

27. *Why are flamingos pink?* https://www.sciencefocus.com/nature/why-are-flamingos-pink/

28. *Jellyfish evaporate in the sun* http://explore-knowmore.blogspot.com/2014/01/jelly-fish-evaporate-in-sun.html

29. *Bladder* https://simple.wikipedia.org/wiki/Bladder

30. *Octopus* https://en.wikipedia.org/wiki/Octopus

31. *These Animals Spawn the Most Offspring in One Go* https://www.nationalgeographic.com/news/2017/04/animals-with-most-offspring-fish-eggs-reproduction/

32. *What Happens to Gorillas on the Pill* https://sciencelife.uchospitals.edu/2011/06/27/what-happens-to-gorillas-on-the-pill/

33. *The Pigeons Nesting, Mating and Feeding Habits* https://www.wild-bird-watching.com/Pigeons.html

34. *Tiger Facts* https://www.nationalgeographic.com.au/animals/tiger-facts.aspx

35. *Do elephants make alarm call that means 'humans!'?* https://earthsky.org/earth/do-elephants-make-alarm-call-that-means-humans

36. *How many species on Earth? About 8.7 million, new estimate says* https://www.sciencedaily.com/releases/2011/08/110823180459.htm

37. *How many plant species are there in the world? Scientists now have an answer* https://news.mongabay.com/2016/05/many-plants-world-scientists-may-now-answer/

38. *Some Monkeys Are (Really) Monogamous* https://www.livescience.com/44791-monkeys-monogamy.html

39. *Castoreum* https://en.wikipedia.org/wiki/Castoreum

40. *Why Do Our Fingers and Toes Wrinkle During a Bath?* https://www.scientificamerican.com/article/why-do-our-fingers-and-toes-wrinkle-during-a-bath/

41. *Do babies have kneecaps* https://www.healthline.com/health/do-babies-have-kneecaps#kneecaps-at-birth

42. *13 amazing things animals can do with their bodies* https://www.mnn.com/earth-matters/animals/photos/amazing-animal-abilities/reindeer-eyes-turn-blue

43. *5 owl facts that will amaze you | MNN* https://www.mnn.com/earth-matters/animals/stories/5-owl-facts-that-will-amaze-you

44. *8 Awesome Things You Didn't Know About Sloths* https://www.thedodo.com/8-awesome-things-you-didnt-kno-668962865.html

45. *why are mosquitos attracted to the colour blue than more than any other colour – Iron Zone* https://ironj11.imascientist.org.uk/question/why-are-mosquitos-attracked-to-the-colour-blue-than-more-than-any-other-colour

46. *BBC - Earth News - 'Supercharged' heart pumps blood up a giraffe's neck* http://news.bbc.co.uk/earth/hi/earth_news/newsid_8368000/8368915.stm

47. *Why is wombat poop cube-shaped?* https://www.nationalgeographic.com/animals/2018/11/wombat-poop-cube-why-is-it-square-shaped/

48. *Octopuses Change Color When They Are Feeling Aggressive | Plants And Animals* https://www.labroots.com/trending/plants-and-animals/2386/octopuses-change-color-when-they-are-feeling-aggressive

49. *Your Teeth (for Kids) - Nemours KidsHealth* https://kidshealth.org/en/kids/teeth.html

50. *Are Apples Better than Coffee? : CCE Suffolk County Family Health & Wellness Strengthening Families & Communities* https://blogs.cornell.edu/ccesuffolk-fhw/2015/07/02/are-apples-better-than-coffee/

51. *Will the world ever be all under water? | AMNH* https://www.amnh.org/explore/ology/earth/ask-a-scientist-about-our-environment/will-the-world-ever-be-all-under-water

52. *Mystery of Moth Flight Uncovered* https://www.livescience.com/4338-mystery-moth-flight-uncovered.html

53. *Is it normal for my baby to have hiccups in the womb?* https://www.babycenter.com/404_is-it-normal-for-my-baby-to-have-hiccups-in-the-womb_2647.bc

54. *Study Guide for The Human Body in Health & Disease* — Linda Swisher, Kevin T. Patton, Gary A. Thibodeau

55. *The Human Odyssey: Navigating the Twelve Stages of Life.* — Thomas Armstrong

56. *Clownfish Sex Changes* https://www.businessinsider.com/clownfish-sex-changes-and-finding-nemo-2013-8?IR=T

57. *Interesting Cat Facts* https://www.cats.org.uk/belfast/feature-pages/interesting-cat-facts

58. *Recycling Facts* http://mariettarecycling.org/why.php

59. *Butterfly Kinesiology: Keeping Warm and Staying Aloft - Butterfly Kinesiology | HowStuffWorks* https://animals.howstuffworks.com/insects/butterfly2.htm

60. *Housefly* https://en.wikipedia.org/wiki/Housefly

61. *Hinny* https://en.wikipedia.org/wiki/Hinny

62. *Greenhouse gases are depriving our oceans of oxygen* https://www.unenvironment.org/news-and-stories/story/greenhouse-gases-are-depriving-our-oceans-oxygen

63. *Why Do Cats Meow at Humans?* https://www.psychologytoday.com/us/blog/all-dogs-go-heaven/201809/why-do-cats-meow-humans

64. *20 Things You Didn't Know About... Mosquitoes* https://www.discovermagazine.com/health/20-things-you-didnt-know-about-mosquitoes

65. *The 11 deadliest animals in the US don't include sharks or crocodiles* https://www.businessinsider.com/deadliest-animals-us-dont-include-sharks-crocodiles-dogs-cows-2019-8?IR=T

66. *Do You Weigh Less When the Moon is Above You?* http://ryanmarciniak.com/archives/518

67. *Billions worldwide suffer from major tooth decay* https://www.sciencedaily.com/releases/2013/05/130530111145.htm

68. *Sex change* https://en.wikipedia.org/wiki/Sex_change

69. *Skin Information and Facts* https://www.nationalgeographic.com/science/health-and-human-body/human-body/skin/

70. *This shrimp packs a punch* https://www.sciencenewsforstudents.org/article/shrimp-packs-punch

71. *How Do Giraffes Mate?* https://sciencing.com/giraffes-mate-4565765.html

72. *What Animal Has the Longest Pregnancy?* https://www.livescience.com/33086-what-animal-has-the-longest-pregnancy.html

73. *The Science Behind Honey's Eternal Shelf Life* https://www.smithsonianmag.com/science-nature/the-science-behind-honeys-eternal-shelf-life-1218690/

74. *Evidence for a midlife crisis in great apes consistent with the U-shape in human well-being* https://www.pnas.org/content/109/49/19949

75. *Alpaca Facts* http://www.starlinealpacas.com.au/alpaca-facts

76. *The Technology That Will Finally Stop Poachers* https://www.popularmechanics.com/science/animals/a25174825/technology-stops-poachers/

77. *Tripod stance* https://en.wikipedia.org/wiki/Tripod_stance

78. *Space Images | Australia's Great Barrier Reef* https://www.jpl.nasa.gov/spaceimages/details.php?id=PIA03401

79. *Hummingbird Facts* https://www.worldofhummingbirds.com/facts.php

80. *Animal and Insect Blood That Isn't Red* https://www.thoughtco.com/animals-with-blue-or-yellow-blood-3975999

81. *Milady's Standard Cosmetology, 2008.* Milady

82. *Can You Grow Apples From Seeds?* https://www.thespruce.com/can-you-grow-apples-from-seeds-3269511

83. *Pigs as Smart as Chimps, Study Says* https://www.seeker.com/iq-tests-suggest-pigs-are-smart-as-dogs-chimps-1769934406.html

84. *Animal Names* https://web.archive.org/web/20150320071411/http://www.npwrc.usgs.gov/about/faqs/animals/names.htm

85. *Polar Bear (Ursus maritimus)* http://www.wwf.ca/conservation/arctic/wildlife/polar_bear/

86. *How much water can a camel store in its hump?* https://wtamu.edu/~cbaird/sq/2013/09/18/how-much-water-can-a-camel-store-in-its-hump/

87. *Exploring the DromeDairy: Camels and Their Milk* https://blogs.scientificamerican.com/guest-blog/exploring-the-dromedairy-camels-and-their-milk/

88. *Tiger Facts* https://www.nationalgeographic.com.au/animals/tiger-facts.aspx

89. *Is Bubonic Plague Still Lurking?* https://www.livescience.com/40003-plague-still-afflicts-world.html

90. *Weight of a Hummingbird | Animals* https://animals.mom.me/weight-hummingbird-3660.html

91. *Blowhole (anatomy)* https://en.wikipedia.org/wiki/Blowhole_(anatomy)

92. *Chameleon spit is 400 times thicker than human's* https://www.sciencemag.org/news/2016/06/chameleon-spit-400-times-thicker-humans

93. *49-Million-Year-Old Cockroach Fossil Found* https://www.livescience.com/42351-european-cockroach-fossils.html

94. *Bird's Eye View* https://www.nationalgeographic.org/media/birds-eye-view-wbt/

95. *PROSTATE CANCER -The James Buchanan Brady Urological Institute* https://urology.jhu.edu/newsletter/prostate_cancer511.php

96. *Animal Facts: Turkeys* https://www.kidzone.ws/animals/turkey.htm

97. *Starfish (Sea Stars)* https://www.nationalgeographic.com/animals/invertebrates/group/starfish/

98. *Why Birds Fly in a V Formation* https://www.sciencemag.org/news/2014/01/why-birds-fly-v-formation

99. *Female glowworms with brighter lights found to attract more mates and to produce more offspring* https://phys.org/news/2015-10-female-glowworms-brighter-offspring.html

100. *3-D Scans Reveal Caterpillars Turning Into Butterflies* https://www.national-geographic.com/science/phenomena/2013/05/14/3-d-scans-caterpillars-transforming-butterflies-metamorphosis/

101. *Blue Whale* https://www.nationalgeographic.com/animals/mammals/b/blue-whale/

102. *Why Do Cats Sleep So Much? 5 Facts About Sleeping Cats* https://www.catster.com/cat-behavior/why-do-cats-sleep-so-much-sleeping-cats-facts

103. *Honey Bee Facts* https://www.sherbornebees.org/honeybee

104. *Camel Humps and Other Water-saving Tactics* https://animals.howstuffworks.com/mammals/camel-go-without-water1.htm

105. *Lobster Facts* http://www.lobstermanspage.net/lobstrs/lfacts.jsp

106. *Maned Wolf Pee Demystified* https://www.wired.com/2011/03/maned-wolf-pee-demystified/

107. *Africa's deforestation twice world rate, says atlas* https://www.reuters.com/article/us-africa-environment/africas-deforestation-twice-world-rate-says-atlas-idUSL1064180420080610

108. *The Water in You: Water and the Human Body* https://www.usgs.gov/special-topic/water-science-school/science/water-you-water-and-human-body?qt-science_center_objects=0#qt-science_center_objects

109. *We May Finally Know Why Giant Beavers Didn't Survive The Ice Age* https://www.iflscience.com/plants-and-animals/we-may-finally-know-why-giant-beavers-didnt-survive-the-ice-age/

110. *Bamboo* https://en.wikipedia.org/wiki/Bamboo

111. *Do Dogs Understand What They Are Seeing on Television?* https://www.psychology-today.com/us/blog/canine-corner/201106/do-dogs-understand-what-they-are-seeing-television

112. *Surgeons find fir tree 'growing inside patient's lung'* https://www.telegraph.co.uk/news/worldnews/europe/russia/5152953/Surgeons-find-fir-tree-growing-inside-patients-lung.html

113. *Why do stingrays and other aquatic creatures leap through the air?* https://slate.com/news-and-politics/2008/03/why-do-stingrays-and-other-aquatic-creatures-leap-through-the-air.html

114. *Short-Horned Lizard* https://www.nationalgeographic.com/animals/reptiles/s/short-horned-lizard/

115. *Dust Mites* http://www.ehso.com/ehshome/dustmites.php

World Geography & Culture

On Earth there are over 7 billion people. That's a lot of us! So naturally, a huge range of cultures and customs have developed across our 196 countries and seven continents. We all live very different lives despite sharing the same planet.

Half of the world's population live on a staple diet of rice.

• • •

Sheep outnumber people 6-1 in New Zealand.

• • •

In 2019, restaurant sales of meat alternatives rose by 268% in the US.

• • •

The main religions of Japan are Shinto and Buddhism, although religion does not play a part in the lives of most Japanese people anymore.

Due to the International Date Line, Samoa is 24 hours ahead of American Samoa despite being only 43 miles apart.

• • •

In Taiwan, garbage trucks play music to remind people to bring out their trash, kind of like an ice cream truck.

• • •

Measured from the centre of Earth, Mount Chimborazo in Ecuador is higher than Mount Everest. Mauna Kea in Hawaii is also taller than Everest using this method.

In Vatican City, every person drinks an average of 105 bottles of wine a year — more than any other country in the world.

• • •

There is only one ATM machine in Antarctica, installed by Wells Fargo in 1998 at McMurdo Station.

• • •

One-third of seafood products in America are mislabelled, so you may not be eating what you think you are.

The average American lives no more than 18 miles from their mom.

• • •

There is a train between Germany and Denmark, which gets on a ship and off again at its destination. It is called Vogelfluglinie in German and Fugleflugtslinjen in Danish.

• • •

Starting on 1 January 2020, France banned the use of three single-use plastic products: cotton ear buds, plates and cups. On 1 January 2021, plastic cutlery and straws will be banned.

Quito in Ecuador is said to have the world's most pleasant climate. It is nicknamed the 'Land of Eternal Spring'.

• • •

The state sport of Maryland is jousting. In fact, it was the first US state to adopt an official sport.

• • •

The last country to outlaw slavery was Mauritania — in 1981.

• • •

The Spanish national anthem has no words. The anthems of Bosnia and Herzegovina, Kosovo and San Marino also have no words.

The Hawaiian alphabet has only 12 letters.

• • •

There's a museum of 'Broken Relationships' in Croatia.

• • •

The Pirahã tribe of North Western Brazil has 8 consonants and 3 vowels in its language.

• • •

Banknotes in Australia are waterproof.

• • •

The longest river in the world is the Nile. It is 4,135 miles long.

More than 600,000 commuters pass through New York's Penn Station every single day, making it the busiest transit hub in the Western Hemisphere.

• • •

There are spas in Austria filled only with warm beer.

• • •

In 1965 there were 180,000 nuns in the USA; now there are only 50,000.

• • •

In France, a Bachelor's degree will cost you €170 a year, even for international students.

There are only two countries in the world that don't offer compulsory paid maternity leave — the USA and Papua New Guinea.

• • •

The line that separates the dark and light sides of the moon is called The Lunar Terminator.

• • •

Mormons believe that the United States' constitution is a divinely inspired document.

• • •

The most common first name in the world is Muhammad (and its multiple spellings).

The capital of Liberia — Monrovia — was named after U.S. President James Monroe.

• • •

The Democratic Republic of Congo has the highest concentration of French speakers outside of France. It is also the highest populated country that has French as its official language — more than France, in fact!

• • •

Mexico has more North American immigrants than from any other country.

• • •

Children with authoritarian parents are more likely to grow up to be Republicans.

President John Quincy Adams loved to skinny dip in the Potomac River.

• • •

In Japan, it is considered rude if you tip a waiter.

• • •

In 2019, Iceland was named as the most peaceful place on Earth by the Institute for Economics and Peace for the 8th year in a row.

• • •

Approximately 6.7% of the U.S. population over 18 years of age has depression.

Around 30-50% of food produced in the world is thrown away.

• • •

There is a pizza vending machine in Italy — it can deliver custom pizzas in 3 minutes.

• • •

Since 2013, the number of airline passengers has more than doubled.

• • •

In Sardinia, there is a type of cheese that contains live maggots. It is called casu marzu.

The world's deepest mailbox is in Susami Bay, Japan, where it is 10 meters underwater.

• • •

In Japan, there is a festival celebrating the penis. It is called Kanamara Matsuri.

• • •

If the entire population of the world was moved to the USA, the country's population density would still be lower than that of Bangladesh.

• • •

Nauru, an island in the Pacific, is the only country in the world not to have an official capital.

The shortest verse in the Bible has just two words: "Jesus Wept" (John 11:35).

• • •

30 percent of the Earth's Uranium supply is in Australia.

• • •

About 90% of the world's population lives in the northern hemisphere.

• • •

The shortest distance between the USA and Russia is only 55 miles — by way of the Bering Strait.

Grüner Lee — a beautiful park in Austria — is submerged by over 30 feet of water during the spring, when the snow melts.

• • •

There is a lizard in Kenya nicknamed the Spider-Lizard as it looks just like Spiderman, with blue and red colorings. It's real name is the Red-headed Rock Agama

• • •

Antarctica doesn't follow a time zone. Scientists who temporarily live there tend to follow the timezone in their home country.

Over 3 billion people live on less than $2.50 a day (in USD using purchasing parity power), which is roughly half of the world's population.

• • •

North Korea and Finland are technically only separated by one country (Russia).

• • •

A study found that video games may help lower the risk of depression.

• • •

One of the world's most expensive hotel is in Jaipur, India where the presidential suite costs $45,000 USD per night.

Before it was colonized, Africa had over 10,000 different states and groups.

• • •

King Edward Point, the capital of South Georgia and the Sandwich Islands, has the lowest population of any capital in the world — just 22.

• • •

Only 9 percent of all plastic waste ever produced has been recycled.

• • •

One third of the entire lava erupted on Earth over the last 500 years has come from volcanoes in Iceland.

In Japan, you can get QR codes on your gravestone so that mourners can access information about the deceased on their cell phone.

• • •

In Sedona, Arizona the golden arches at McDonald's are actually turquoise, to fit in with the relaxing atmosphere of the place.

• • •

The only religious buildings in Antarctica are churches.

• • •

Alaska is the northernmost, easternmost and westernmost state in the USA. This is because parts of Alaska's Aleutian Islands cross over the 180° line of longitude, making it the easternmost state.

There is a museum in Croatia called "Froggyland", which is entirely composed of over 500 stuffed frogs in human position.

• • •

The tiny country of Bangladesh has a larger population than Russia.

• • •

A 250-year old Banyan tree in Kolkata, India is bigger than the average WalMart.

• • •

The Mexican sombrero hat is designed very wide to be able to provide shade to the entire body.

In Italy, a man may be arrested for wearing a skirt.

• • •

Coffee beans aren't beans. They're fruit pits.

• • •

Every Alaskan citizen over the age of six months receives an oil dividend check of between around $300-2000 per year.

• • •

In Thailand, people text 555 to each other instead of hahaha, because the number 5 is pronounced 'ha' in Thai.

In Japan, there are white strawberries with red seeds called 'The Scent of First Love'. They are very expensive to buy, but are popular as wedding and birthday gifts.

• • •

Sequoia National Park in California contains the world's largest living tree — its trunk is 102 feet in circumference.

• • •

Burj Khalifa — the tallest building in the world — was built by Samsung.

• • •

In Armenia, Christmas Eve is on the 5th January.

The top of the Eiffel Tower leans away from the sun as the metal that is facing the sun expands upwards as it heats.

• • •

All the Giant Pandas in the world are owned by China. This means that any Giant Panda seen in a zoo around the world is actually on 'loan' from China.

• • •

Black ice-cream, made from coconut ash, became very trendy in 2016. However, New York City banned it in 2018 as it posed health risks.

Just 10 years ago, only 500 or so people in China could ski. Now, each year more than five million Chinese people visit ski resorts.

• • •

Dubai imports its sand from Australia.

• • •

As icebergs and glaciers melt they make a fizzing sound known as 'bergy seltzer'.

• • •

Virginia extends 95 miles further west than West Virginia.

There is an opera house on the US-Canada border where the stage is in one country and the audience in another. The Haskell Free Library and Opera House is in both Quebec and Vermont.

• • •

The University of Alaska stretches over four time zones.

• • •

In Antarctica, there is a waterfall that regularly pours out red liquid (it is oxidized salty water), and is known as Blood Falls.

• • •

Denver, Colorado currently has more marijuana dispensaries than McDonald's and Starbucks combined.

Panama is the only place in the world where you can see the sun rise on the Pacific Ocean and set on the Atlantic Ocean.

• • •

Only 10% of people in the world are left-handed.

• • •

The state fish of Hawaii is the humuhumunukunukuapua'a.

• • •

The Tonle Sap River in Cambodia flows southeast to to northwest half of the year, then changes direction the other half.

Around 20% of Ugandans believe in witchcraft.

• • •

There are four different writing systems in Japan: Romaji, Katakana, Hiragana and Kanji.

• • •

Japan is about the same size as California but has half the population of the entire United States.

• • •

In South Korea, planes are banned from landing or taking off during the stressful annual college entrance exams — to ensure students have perfectly silent surroundings.

There are over 200 corpses on Mount Everest. Climbers use them as waypoints on their own ascents.

• • •

In China, it has become a fashion statement to wear face masks, which protect them from pollution. They now come in all sorts of designer colours and styles.

• • •

Until 2011, Russia didn't consider beer to be alcohol — it was classified as a soft drink.

• • •

Niagara Falls can freeze over if it gets cold enough.

There are 180,000 islands in Finland.

• • •

"Live free or die" is the official state slogan of New Hampshire and is written on all license plates. Ironically, prisoners in New Hampshire make the license plates.

• • •

An ice-cream shop in the USA sells black pudding and insect-flavored ice cream.

Sources

1. ***Key facts about rice*** http://www.thenewhumanitarian.org/report/91012/asia-key-facts-about-rice
2. ***New Zealand is home to 3 million people and 60 million sheep*** http://archive.stats.govt.nz/browse_for_stats/population/mythbusters/3million-people-60million-sheep.aspx
3. ***Religion in Japan*** https://www.japan-guide.com/e/e629.html
4. ***Samoa Time Zone*** https://en.wikipedia.org/wiki/Samoa_Time_Zone
5. ***Carl's Jr Beyond BBQ Cheeseburger: New plant-based item arrives Oct. 9*** https://eu.usatoday.com/story/money/food/2019/09/30/world-vegetarian-day-more-meat-free-and-vegan-options-coming/3777627002/
6. ***Taiwan Garbage Trucks: Classical Music Accompanies Collection (VIDEO)*** https://www.huffpost.com/entry/taiwan-garbage-trucks-music_n_1195020
7. ***What is the highest point on Earth as measured from Earth's center?*** https://ocean-service.noaa.gov/facts/highestpoint.html
8. ***Penn Station Is NYC's Commuter Nightmare, and It's About to Get Worse*** https://www.bloomberg.com/graphics/2017-penn-station-summer-construction-creates-commuting-hell/
9. ***International students in France handed court victory over plan to hike tuition fees*** https://www.thelocal.fr/20191014/legal-victory-over-tuition-fees-hike-for-foreign-students-in-france
10. ***Which state drinks more wine per person than anywhere else?*** https://www.independent.co.uk/news/world/europe/vatican-city-drinks-more-wine-per-person-than-anywhere-else-in-the-world-9151475.html
11. ***U.S. nuns face shrinking numbers and tensions with the Vatican*** https://www.pewresearch.org/fact-tank/2014/08/08/u-s-nuns-face-shrinking-numbers-and-tensions-with-the-vatican/
12. ***The World's Loneliest ATM is in Antarctica*** https://www.mentalfloss.com/article/63741/worlds-loneliest-atm-antarctica
13. ***The typical American lives only 18 miles from Mom*** https://www.bostonglobe.com/news/nation/2015/12/24/the-typical-american-lives-only-miles-from-mom/iSYQglkxaqA-0VUe3WWHt7K/story.html
14. ***Vogelfluglinie*** https://en.wikipedia.org/wiki/Vogelfluglinie
15. ***Explainer: Global airlines on high alert as virus outbreak spreads*** https://www.reuters.com/article/us-china-health-travel-explainer/explainer-global-airlines-on-high-alert-as-virus-outbreak-spreads-idUSKBN1ZM0M2

16. *Slavery in Mauritania* https://en.wikipedia.org/wiki/Slavery_in_Mauritania

17. *France to phase out single-use plastics starting January 1* https://www.france24.com/en/20191231-france-begins-phasing-out-single-use-plastics

18. *Our South American Neighbors by G. Southworth* https://www.heritage-history.com/index.php?c=read&author=southworth&book=south&story=ecuador

19. *Developmental Antecedents of Political Ideology: A Longitudinal Investigation From Birth to Age 18 Years - R. Chris Fraley, Brian N. Griffin, Jay Belsky, Glenn I. Roisman, 2012* https://journals.sagepub.com/doi/abs/10.1177/0956797612440102

20. *Fighting Depression: Action Video Game Play May Reduce Rumination and Increase Subjective and Objective Cognition in Depressed Patients* https://www.ncbi.nlm.nih.gov/pmc/articles/PMC5816361/

21. *Global Food: Waste Not, Want Not* https://www.imeche.org/policy-and-press/reports/detail/global-food-waste-not-want-not

22. *Sports Why Jousting Is Maryland's Official State Sport* https://theculturetrip.com/north-america/usa/maryland/articles/why-jousting-is-marylands-official-state-sport/

23. *Marcha Real* https://en.wikipedia.org/wiki/Marcha_Real

24. *Hawaiian alphabet* https://en.wikipedia.org/wiki/Hawaiian_alphabet

25. *Museum of Broken Relationships* https://en.wikipedia.org/wiki/Museum_of_Broken_Relationships

26. *Everett on the Pirahã Language of Brazil* https://newlearningonline.com/literacies/chapter-1/everett-on-the-pirahae-language-of-brazil

27. *Australian banknotes: One of the most advanced in the world* https://www.cnbc.com/2018/02/21/australian-banknotes-one-of-the-most-advanced-in-the-world.html

28. *What's the World's Longest River?* https://www.livescience.com/32600-what-is-the-worlds-longest-river.html

29. *The Austrian brewery turned beer spa that lets you bask in gallons of pints* https://www.lonelyplanet.com/articles/worlds-only-beer-spa-in-austria

30. *America is the only rich country without a law on paid leave for new parents* https://www.economist.com/united-states/2019/07/18/america-is-the-only-rich-country-without-a-law-on-paid-leave-for-new-parents

31. *General Astronomy/Phases of the Moon* https://en.wikibooks.org/wiki/General_Astronomy/Phases_of_the_Moon

32. *The Divinely Inspired Constitution* https://www.churchofjesuschrist.org/study/ensign/1992/02/the-divinely-inspired-constitution?lang=eng

33. *Muhammad (name)* https://en.wikipedia.org/wiki/Muhammad_(name)

34. *Monrovia* https://en.wikipedia.org/wiki/Monrovia

35. *The Countries That Speak the Most French (Besides France)* https://frenchly.us/the-countries-outside-of-france-that-speak-the-most-french/

36. *Ice Cream Shop Is Serving Blood And Insect Ice Cream Pints Because Halloween* https://www.foodbeast.com/news/salt-straw-blood-insect-ice-cream/

37. *Immigration to Mexico* https://en.wikipedia.org/wiki/Immigration_to_Mexico#North_American

38. *The Skinny on John Quincy Adams's Skinny Dipping Interview* https://www.ploddingthroughthepresidents.com/2017/02/john-quincy-adams-skinny-dipping.html

39. *#BeatPlasticPollution This World Environment Day* https://www.unenvironment.org/interactive/beat-plastic-pollution/

40. *Do you Tip in Japan? Japanese Tipping Etiquette - InsideJapan Blog* https://www.insidejapantours.com/blog/2013/09/22/do-you-tip-in-japan-japanese-tipping-etiquette/

41. *Iceland tops the charts for most peaceful country in the world* http://www.rfi.fr/en/general/20190611-iceland-most-peaceful-global-peace-index-2019-postitive-negative

42. *Depression* https://www.healthline.com/health/depression/facts-statistics-infographic#1

43. *24-hour pizza vending machine Let's Pizza launches in Italy* https://realbusiness.co.uk/24-hour-pizza-vending-machine-lets-pizza-launches-in-italy/

44. *Casu marzu* https://en.wikipedia.org/wiki/Casu_marzu

45. *Town's undersea mailbox lures divers* https://www.japantimes.co.jp/news/2013/07/26/national/towns-undersea-mailbox-lures-divers/

46. *Kanamara Matsuri* https://en.wikipedia.org/wiki/Kanamara_Matsuri

47. *Population Challenges for Bangladesh in the Coming Decades* https://www.ncbi.nlm.nih.gov/pmc/articles/PMC2740702/

48. *Nauru: The Country Without a Capital* https://www.cntraveler.com/stories/2013-02-04/nauru-country-without-a-capital-maphead-ken-jennings

49. *Jesus wept* https://en.wikipedia.org/wiki/Jesus_wept

50. *Uranium mining in Australia* https://en.wikipedia.org/wiki/Uranium_mining_in_Australia

51. *Northern Hemisphere* https://simple.wikipedia.org/wiki/Northern_Hemisphere

52. *Can you really see Russia from Alaska?* https://slate.com/news-and-politics/2008/09/can-you-really-see-russia-from-alaska.html

53. *Grüner See (Styria)* https://en.wikipedia.org/wiki/Gr%C3%BCner_See_(Styria)

54. *Field Guide: Red-headed Rock Agama | MpalaLive* http://mpalalive.org/field_guide/red_headed_rock_agama

55. *What's Antarctica's time zone?* https://www.hurtigruten.com/destinations/antarctica/inspiration/antarctica-time-zone/

56. *Poverty Facts and Stats* http://www.globalissues.org/article/26/poverty-facts-and-stats

57. *Presidential Suite at Raj Palace from World's Most Expensive Hotel Rooms*

https://www.eonline.com/photos/14050/world-s-most-expensive-hotel-rooms/428116

58. *History of Africa* https://en.wikipedia.org/wiki/History_of_Africa

59. *Volcanology of Iceland* https://en.wikipedia.org/wiki/Volcanology_of_Iceland

60. *QR Codes for the Dead* https://www.theatlantic.com/technology/archive/2014/05/qr-codes-for-the-dead/370901/

61. *Why This Arizona McDonald's Uses Turquoise Instead of Golden Arches* https://www.rd.com/food/fun/mcdonalds-turquoise-arches/

62. *Religion in Antarctica* https://en.wikipedia.org/wiki/Religion_in_Antarctica

63. *Aleutian Islands* https://en.wikipedia.org/wiki/Aleutian_Islands

64. *Froggyland Croatia* https://www.tripadvisor.com/Attraction_Review-g295370-d4299371-Reviews-Froggyland-Split_Split_Dalmatia_County_Dalmatia.html

65. *List of countries and dependencies by population* https://en.wikipedia.org/wiki/List_of_countries_and_dependencies_by_population

66. *A Brief History of Kolkata's Great Banyan Tree* https://theculturetrip.com/asia/india/articles/a-brief-history-of-kolkatas-great-banyan-tree/

67. *Sombrero* https://en.wikipedia.org/wiki/Sombrero

68. *Unusual Italian Laws* https://www.italymagazine.com/news/unusual-italian-laws

69. *Coffee bean* https://en.wikipedia.org/wiki/Coffee_bean

70. *Alaska Permanent Fund* https://en.wikipedia.org/wiki/Alaska_Permanent_Fund

71. *55555, or, How to Laugh Online in Other Languages* https://www.theatlantic.com/technology/archive/2012/12/55555-or-how-to-laugh-online-in-other-languages/266175/

72. *White strawberries: Scent of First Love* https://japantoday.com/category/features/food/white-strawberries-scent-of-first-love

73. *Giant Sequoias and Redwoods: The Largest and Tallest Trees* https://www.livescience.com/39461-sequoias-redwood-trees.html

74. *Burj Khalifa* https://en.wikipedia.org/wiki/Burj_Khalifa

75. *It's Still Christmas in Armenia | Travel* https://www.smithsonianmag.com/travel/its-still-christmas-armenia-180967689/

76. *20 Interesting Facts Most People Don't Know* https://www.bloomsbury-international.com/blog/2017/08/11/20-interesting-facts/

77. *Giant pandas around the world* https://en.wikipedia.org/wiki/Giant_pandas_around_the_world

78. *Coconut Ash still trending in China despite New York banned* https://news.cgtn.com/news/3d3d414d3345444f78457a6333566d54/share_p.html

79. *How the Olympics Turned China on to Skiing* https://www.outsideonline.com/2273766/chinese-downhill

80. *Why even Arab nations are buying sand* https://timesofindia.indiatimes.com/world/middle-east/why-even-arab-nations-are-buying-sand/articleshow/60492513.cms

81. *Bergy Seltzer* https://www.gi.alaska.edu/alaska-science-forum/bergy-seltzer

82. *Virginia extends farther west than West Virginia* https://americanprofile.com/articles/virginia-extends-farther-west-than-west-virginia/

83. *Haskell Free Library and Opera House* https://en.wikipedia.org/wiki/Haskell_Free_Library_and_Opera_House

84. *Time Zones* https://www.gi.alaska.edu/alaska-science-forum/time-zones

85. *Blood Falls* https://en.wikipedia.org/wiki/Blood_Falls

86. *How Many Dispensaries in Denver, Colorado? We Counted Them.* https://my-420tours.com/many-dispensaries-denver-colorado/

87. *Fun Facts* https://www.embassyofpanama.org/fun-facts

88. *Handedness* https://en.wikipedia.org/wiki/Handedness

89. *Reef triggerfish* https://en.wikipedia.org/wiki/Reef_triggerfish

90. *Tonlé Sap* https://en.wikipedia.org/wiki/Tonl%C3%A9_Sap

91. *Six million Ugandans believe in witchcraft- report* https://www.monitor.co.ug/News/National/688334-902622-bt1n72z/index.html

92. *The Ultimate Guide to Japanese Writing Systems: Learning to Read Hiragana, Katakana and Kanji* http://eurolinguiste.com/japanese-writing-systems/

93. *SPEAK*. Rudolph F. Verderber

94. *Suneung: The day silence falls over South Korea* https://www.bbc.com/news/world-asia-46181240

95. *There Are Over 200 Bodies on Mount Everest, And They're Used as Landmarks* https://www.smithsonianmag.com/smart-news/there-are-over-200-bodies-on-mount-everest-and-theyre-used-as-landmarks-146904416/

96. *How did the face mask - a symbol of Hong Kong's anti-extradition bill protest - become a fashion accessory?* https://www.scmp.com/magazines/style/news-trends/article/3025902/how-did-face-mask-hong-kongs-anti-extradition-bill

97. *Russia Decides Beer is Alcohol, not Food* https://www.ibtimes.com/russia-decides-beer-alcohol-not-food-300825

98. *How Cold Is It in Canada? Niagara Falls Has Frozen Over* https://www.mentalfloss.com/article/571434/how-cold-it-canada-niagara-falls-has-frozen-over

99. *The land of the hundred thousand lakes and islands* https://sail-in-finland.info/2012/07/finland-the-land-of-the-hundred-thousand-lakes-and-islands/

100. *Live Free or Die* https://en.wikipedia.org/wiki/Live_Free_or_Die

Business & Politics

Business and politics shape the world — often in a good way, sometimes in a bad way. There's no denying that some of the world's biggest companies such as Apple and Microsoft have changed our lives. Let's learn more about some of the big players in the world of business and politics.

Bill Clinton met President Kennedy in the White House Rose Garden when he was a young boy in 1963.

• • •

It is estimated that 94 per cent of the world's population recognize Coke's red and white logo.

• • •

Every day, 15% of the searches that occur are ones that Google has never seen before.

• • •

The company Adobe was named after the Adobe Creek that ran behind the house of co-founder John Warnock.

One in eight Americans have at one point been employed by McDonald's.

• • •

Every year, every manager at Amazon spends two days doing call-centre training — even the CEO.

• • •

Everyone that works at Ben & Jerry's headquarters can take home three pints of ice cream every single day that they work.

• • •

The name Reebok is a stylized version of the word rhebok — an African antelope.

Founded in 930, the Parliament of Iceland is the oldest acting parliament in the world.

• • •

If you have $10 in your pocket and no debt, you are wealthier than 25% of Americans.

• • •

Karl Marx was once a correspondent for the New York Daily Tribune.

• • •

After Donald Trump was elected in 2016, New Zealand's immigration website received 17,000 registrations of interest in one month from Americans wanting to emigrate there. They normally receive around 3,000 registrations from Americans per month.

Up until 1910, Bayer — the company that produces health products including aspirin — sold heroine as a medicine for children suffering from coughs and colds.

• • •

Hewlett Packard, Apple and Microsoft were all started in a garage.

• • •

Steve Jobs was an executive producer on Toy Story.

• • •

The first menu item at McDonald's was a hot dog, not hamburgers.

During the war in Iraq and Afghanistan, the U.S. Military spent over $20 billion a year on air conditioning — more than NASA's total budget.

• • •

The first five U.S. Presidents were never photographed.

• • •

Disney owns 80% of ESPN.

• • •

Ronald Reagan was a lifeguard during high school and saved 77 people's lives.

Kim Jong II allegedly wrote six operas that were better than any in the history of music, according to his official biography.

• • •

The biggest selling product of all time is the Rubik's cube. It is followed by the iPhone.

• • •

Mark Zuckerberg is red-green color blind, which is why Facebook is so blue.

• • •

In 2019, the retail industry spent the most money on television advertising than any other industry.

Pennsylvania is misspelled on both the Liberty Bell and on the US Constitution. It is missing an 'n'.

• • •

At 4,400 words, the US Constitution is the shortest constitution of any major government.

• • •

If you smoke near an Apple computer, you void its warranty.

• • •

Warner Music owns the copyright to 'Happy Birthday'.

Around 70 percent of small businesses are owned and operated by a single person.

• • •

Over 84 million 'mouse ears' have been sold at Walt Disney World since it opened.

• • •

You can purchase large sheets of uncut US currency through the mail at moneyfactory.gov.

• • •

On Instagram, a study found that warm, high-contrast filters like Mayfair generate the most likes.

Over one-third of the US population visits WalMart each week.

• • •

Bill Gates is wealthier than the GDP of 122 countries.

• • •

20 percent of South Korea's gross domestic product comes from Samsung.

• • •

Starbucks brought in round tables so that customers would feel less alone.

Ben & Jerry's ice cream is owned by Unilever, which also makes deodorant.

. . .

One in 10 Europeans are conceived on an Ikea bed.

. . .

Google was originally called BackRub.

. . .

Some things you say to Siri on your iPhone are stored and analyzed by Apple. However, the data is anonymous.

Modern Thanksgiving was originally thought up by George Washington to give thanks to the Constitution.

• • •

The founder of FedEx once saved the company by taking its final $5,000 and gambling it in Las Vegas for a huge profit.

• • •

The YKK on zippers stands for Yoshida Kogyo Kabushiki Kaisha. The company makes around 90 per cent of all zippers in the world. Their largest factory is in Georgia and it makes over seven million zippers a day.

It is estimated that US corporations are hiding over $1.6 trillion of profits in offshore accounts.

• • •

Apple iPhone screens are mostly made by Samsung.

• • •

If it were made in America, the iPhone would cost $2,000.

• • •

Topeka, Kansas changed its name to 'Google' in 2010 to try and get the attention of Google executives who were selecting communities for a trial run of its new Google Fiber network.

Every single hour, WalMart brings in over $1.8 million of profit.

• • •

Swedish automobile manufacturer, Volvo, which has a focus on safety, gave away its patent to the three-point seat belt in order to save lives.

• • •

Lego is the biggest producer of rubber tires in the world.

• • •

Dell Computers was started by a 19-year-old with only $1,000.

Google's old motto used to be 'Don't be evil'.
They dropped it in 2015, but it is still part of their
corporate code of conduct.

• • •

When he was 17, Elon Musk lived off one dollar a
day for a month to see if he would be able to make
it as an entrepreneur.

• • •

The actor who played the Marlboro Man in the
famous ads died of lung cancer.

• • •

In Texas, death row inmates no longer get to
choose their last meal.

In 1984, the New Zealand Prime Minister called a spontaneous general election while he was drunk. He lost.

• • •

Steve Wozniak was so good at Tetris — he was the #1 player in the USA for many years — he got banned from submitting his scores to Nintendo Power magazine.

• • •

President James Madison was Princeton's first grad student.

• • •

Nintendo originally started out by producing playing cards.

The grave of Karl Marx has an entrance fee.

• • •

People in the USA get so excited about food during the Super Bowl that the sale of antacids increases by 20% every year after the day of the game.

• • •

The founder of Guinness Brewery had 21 children with his one wife.

• • •

During the 8 years that Bill Clinton was President, he only sent two emails.

There are more people on Facebook than there were on Earth 200 years ago.

• • •

The homewares company, IKEA, is actually registered as a 'not for profit', due to a claim that they are advancing architecture and interior design.

• • •

When George W. Bush was 30 years old, he was arrested for driving under the influence of alcohol.

• • •

A Tupperware party starts somewhere in the world every 23 seconds.

In 2016, hackers managed to break into Mark Zuckerberg's Twitter and Pinterest accounts. They claimed his password was 'dadada'.

• • •

It costs the U.S. Mint nearly twice as much to produce new penny and nickel coins than they are worth.

• • •

About 4.6% of the population of New York City has a net worth of over $1 million. Meaning that one out of every 21 New Yorkers is a millionaire.

• • •

Every day, around 10,000 Facebook users die. Meaning that dead Facebook users will soon outnumber living ones.

Uber, the world's largest taxi provider, owns no vehicles of its own.

• • •

One of the chief exports of Nauru, a small island in the Western Pacific, is fossilized bird droppings (also known as phosphate).

• • •

Milton Hershey left almost his entire fortune to fund the Milton Hershey School, which was originally for orphan boys but is now open for boys and girls from over 30 states.

• • •

In 2006, the term 'to Google' was recognized by the Merriam Webster dictionary and the Oxford English Dictionary.

Google has a Klingon interface.

• • •

During the Cold War, U.S. spies were caught by the KGB because they used high-quality American staples in their fake Soviet passports, instead of Russian ones, which would rust.

• • •

The most dangerous job in the United States is a fisherman, with 116 deaths per 10,000 workers. This is followed by logging and garbage collection.

• • •

Starbucks spends more on healthcare insurance for its employees than it does on coffee beans.

The bloodhound is the only animal whose evidence is admissible in an American court.

• • •

At the movie theatre, $30 of raw popcorn translates into $3,000 worth of sales.

• • •

Donald Trump launched his own brand of vodka, but it didn't sell very well. Maybe it's because he claims to never have had a sip of alcohol!

• • •

Milton Hershey built the town of Hershey in Pennsylvania so that his employees could create a community where they could be self-reliant and own their own homes.

George Washington did not sign the Declaration of Independence. He was already in New York commanding troops when the Declaration was adopted.

Sources

1. *Bill Clinton and John F. Kennedy: The Story Behind Their 1963 Handshake* https://www.biography.com/news/john-f-kennedy-bill-clinton-handshake-1963
2. *Who We Are* https://www.coca-colacompany.com/careers/who-we-are
3. *Google reaffirms 15% of searches are new, never been searched before* https://searchengineland.com/google-reaffirms-15-searches-new-never-searched-273786
4. *Adobe Inc.* https://en.wikipedia.org/wiki/Adobe_Inc.
5. *11 things about McDonald's that may surprise you* https://www.cbsnews.com/media/11-things-about-mcdonalds-that-may-surprise-you/
6. *7 Customer Service Lessons from Amazon CEO Jeff Bezos* https://www.salesforce.com/blog/2013/06/jeff-bezos-lessons.html
7. *Reebok* https://en.wikipedia.org/wiki/Reebok
8. *What's the best part about working at Ben & Jerry's? | Ben* https://www.benjerry.com/flavors/3-pints-a-day
9. *Althing* https://en.wikipedia.org/wiki/Althing
10. *Credit Suisse: with just $10 "you're wealthier than 25% of Americans"* https://www.sovereignman.com/trends/credit-suisse-with-just-10-youre-wealthier-than-25-of-americans-18072/
11. *New-York Tribune* https://en.wikipedia.org/wiki/New-York_Tribune
12. *Bayer* https://en.wikipedia.org/wiki/Bayer
13. *6 $25 Billion Companies That Started in a Garage* https://www.inc.com/drew-hendricks/6-25-billion-companies-that-started-in-a-garage.html
14. *Steve Jobs* https://pixar.fandom.com/wiki/Steve_Jobs
15. *US Migration to New Zealand Up in 2017 After Trump Election* https://fortune.com/2018/02/02/us-migration-new-zealand-trump/
16. *Dick and Mac McDonald - How McDonald's Works | HowStuffWorks* https://money.howstuffworks.com/mcdonalds1.htm
17. *Among The Costs Of War: Billions A Year In A.C.?* https://www.npr.org/2011/06/25/137414737/among-the-costs-of-war-20b-in-air-conditioning
18. *Which American President Was the First to be Photographed?* https://www.history.com/news/john-quincy-adams-early-photo
19. *Disney's Top Companies and Brands* https://www.investopedia.com/articles/markets/102915/top-5-companies-owned-disney.asp
20. *Ronald Reagan Timeline* https://www.npr.org/news/specials/obits/reagan/timeline.html

21. *The Strange Musical World of Kim Jong Il | WQXR Blog* https://www.wqxr.org/story/176557-strange-musical-world-kim-jong-il/

22. *10 best-selling products of all time* https://eu.usatoday.com/story/money/business/2014/05/18/24-7-wall-st-the-best-selling-products-of-all-time/9223465/

23. *10 surprising facts about Mark Zuckerberg* https://www.washingtonpost.com/business/technology/10-surprising-facts-about-mark-zuckerberg/2012/05/30/gJQAJ9yJ2U_story.html

24. *Biggest TV Advertisers Spent Almost $10 Billion in 2019* https://www.adweek.com/tv-video/televisions-biggest-advertisers-spent-almost-10-billion-in-2019/

25. *Pennsylvania is spelled wrong in the Constitution: 11 fun facts for Constitution Day* https://www.pennlive.com/opinion/2015/09/us_constitution_fun_facts.html

26. *The Constitution Curse: and other facts you didn't know about the Constitution* https://www.onelegal.com/blog/the-constitution-curse-and-other-facts-you-didnt-know-about-the-constitution/

27. *Apple voids Applecare warranty for smokers!* https://www.computerworld.com/article/2468226/apple-voids-applecare-warranty-for-smokers-.html

28. *Happy Birthday to You* https://en.wikipedia.org/wiki/Happy_Birthday_to_You

29. *Business Insider* https://www.businessinsider.com/facts-about-small-businesses-in-america-2011-8?IR=T

30. *23 crazy facts about Disneyland* https://www.businessinsider.com/23-crazy-facts-about-disneyland-2015-7?IR=T

31. *Buying, Selling, & Redeeming* https://www.treasury.gov/resource-center/faqs/Currency/Pages/edu_faq_currency_sales.aspx

32. *The Best Instagram Filter To Get The Most Likes, Says Study* https://www.yourtango.com/2016291359/best-instagram-filter-to-get-most-likes-says-science

33. *The Grocery List: Why 140 Million Americans Choose Walmart* https://corporate.walmart.com/newsroom/business/20161003/the-grocery-list-why-140-million-americans-choose-walmart

34. *Wealth of the World's Richest People vs GDP of Countries* https://knoema.com/wqezguc/wealth-of-the-world-s-richest-people-vs-gdp-of-countries

35. *How Samsung dominates South Korea's economy* https://money.cnn.com/2017/02/17/technology/samsung-south-korea-daily-life/index.html

36. I Starbucks: Round Tables At Starbucks Are They Designed To Make People Feel Less Lonely? https://www.foodworldnews.com/articles/15813/20150304/starbucks-round-tables-designed-make-feel-less-lonely.htm

37. *List of Unilever brands* https://en.wikipedia.org/wiki/List_of_Unilever_brands

38. *One in Ten Europeans Were Conceived in IKEA Beds* https://www.theatlantic.com/international/archive/2011/09/one-ten-europeans-were-conceived-ikea-beds/337380/

39. *Google was originally called BackRub* https://gizmodo.com/google-was-originally-called-backrub-1605435217

40. *Apple contractors 'regularly hear confidential details' on Siri recordings* https://www.theguardian.com/technology/2019/jul/26/apple-contractors-regularly-hear-confidential-details-on-siri-recordings

41. *Thanksgiving · George* https://www.mountvernon.org/library/digitalhistory/digital-encyclopedia/article/thanksgiving/

42. *Frederick W. Smith* https://en.wikipedia.org/wiki/Frederick_W._Smith

43. *YKK* https://en.wikipedia.org/wiki/YKK

44. *Companies of the United States with untaxed profits* https://en.wikipedia.org/wiki/Companies_of_the_United_States_with_untaxed_profits

45. *Does Samsung Make iPhone Parts?* https://itstillworks.com/samsung-make-iphone-parts-18028.html

46. *How Much Would a 'Made in America' iPhone Cost? Too Much. | Mark J. Perry* https://fee.org/articles/a-made-in-america-iphone-would-cost-2-000-studies-show/

47. *How Google Fiber Changed Kansas City | Here & Now* https://www.wbur.org/here-andnow/2017/11/08/google-fiber-kansas-city

48. *Walmart SWOT analysis 2019 | SWOT Analysis of Walmart* https://bstrategyhub.com/swot-analysis-of-walmart-2019-walmart-swot-analysis/

49. *A MILLION LIVES SAVED SINCE VOLVO INVENTED THE THREE-POINT SAFETY BELT* https://www.media.volvocars.com/uk/en-gb/media/pressreleases/20505

50. *Lego tire* https://en.wikipedia.org/wiki/Lego_tire

51. *How Michael Dell turned $1,000 into billions, starting from his dorm* https://www.cnbc.com/2018/02/26/how-michael-dell-turned-1000-into-billions-starting-from-his-dorm.html

52. *Don't be evil* https://en.wikipedia.org/wiki/Don%27t_be_evil

53. *Elon Musk living off a dollar a day StarTalk* https://www.businessinsider.com/elon-musk-living-off-a-dollar-a-day-startalk-2015-3?IR=T

54. *Marlboro Man* https://en.wikipedia.org/wiki/Marlboro_Man

55. *Last meal* https://en.wikipedia.org/wiki/Last_meal

56. *1984 New Zealand general election* https://en.wikipedia.org/wiki/1984_New_Zealand_general_election

57. *Steve Wozniak Was So Good at Tetris He Got Banned from Nintendo Power* https://gizmodo.com/steve-wozniak-was-once-the-best-tetris-player-in-americ-1587220552

58. *10 Things You May Not Know About James Madison* https://www.history.com/news/10-things-you-may-not-know-about-james-madison

59. *The Extraordinary and Surprising History of Nintendo* https://interestingengi-

neering.com/the-extraordinary-and-surprising-history-of-nintendo

60. *Das Tomb: Karl Marx's Grave Has an Entry Fee* https://www.theatlantic.com/business/archive/2015/10/das-tomb-karl-marxs-resting-place-has-an-entry-fee/412411/

61. *Super Bowl Sunday Diet Tips: The Second-Biggest Eating Holiday of the Year* https://www.shape.com/healthy-eating/diet-tips/super-bowl-food-shockers-you-wont-believe

62. *Arthur Guinness* https://en.wikipedia.org/wiki/Arthur_Guinness

63. *The Truth About Bill Clinton's Emails* https://www.theatlantic.com/technology/archive/2015/03/the-myth-about-bill-clintons-emails/387604/

64. *World Population Growth* https://ourworldindata.org/world-population-growth

65. *Is IKEA the World's Largest Charity?* https://www.mentalfloss.com/article/18575/ikea-worlds-largest-charity

66. *Early life of George W. Bush* https://en.wikipedia.org/wiki/Early_life_of_George_W._Bush

67. *Tupperware: How the 1950s party model conquered the world* https://www.bbc.com/news/business-38880964

68. *Mark Zuckerberg's Twitter, Pinterest hacked after LinkedIn breach* https://www.businessinsider.com/mark-zuckerberg-twitter-pinterest-accounts-hacked-linkedin-hack-facebook-passwords-2016-6?IR=T

69. *Pennies and nickels cost more to make than they're worth* https://money.cnn.com/2016/01/11/news/economy/u-s-coins/index.html

70. *New York City is home to nearly 1 million millionaires, more than any other city in the world* https://www.cnbc.com/2019/01/18/new-york-city-has-more-millionaires-than-any-other-city-in-the-world.html

71. *Dead Facebook users will soon outnumber the living* https://www.theloop.ca/dead-facebook-users-will-soon-outnumber-the-living/

72. *The Battle Is For The Customer Interface* https://techcrunch.com/2015/03/03/in-the-age-of-disintermediation-the-battle-is-all-for-the-customer-interface/

73. *Economy of Nauru* https://en.wikipedia.org/wiki/Economy_of_Nauru

74. *Milton Hershey School* https://en.wikipedia.org/wiki/Milton_Hershey_School

75. *Google (verb)* https://en.wikipedia.org/wiki/Google_(verb)

76. *Google in Klingon* https://www.google.com/?hl=xx-klingon

77. *Europe | Museum exhibits Russia's cold war secrets* http://news.bbc.co.uk/2/hi/europe/2065020.stm

78. *The 10 Most Dangerous Jobs in the United States* https://www.ehstoday.com/safety/article/21917221/the-10-most-dangerous-jobs-in-the-united-states

79. *Starbucks spends more on health care than coffee - Jun. 7, 2010* https://archive.fortune.com/2010/06/07/news/companies/starbucks_schultz_healthcare.fortune/index.htm

80. ***First animal whose evidence is admissible in court*** https://www.guinnessworldre-cords.com/world-records/first-animal-whose-evidence-is-admissible-in-court/

81. ***Now Showing: Declining Sales at Theater Snack Bars*** https://www.latimes.com/archives/la-xpm-2006-mar-18-fi-concessions18-story.html

82. ***On the Rocks: The Story of Trump Vodka*** https://www.bloomberg.com/features/2016-trump-vodka/

83. ***Milton S. Hershey*** https://www.hersheypa.com/about-hershey/milton-hershey.php

84. ***9 Things You May Not Know About the Declaration of Independence*** https://www.history.com/news/9-things-you-may-not-know-about-the-declaration-of-independence

History

Earth was civilized by humans (as far as we know) around 200,000 years ago. And before that, our ancestors had been around for about six million years. In fact, modern civilization as we know it is only about 6,000 years old.

However, we've gotten a lot done in those 6,000 years, as these facts will show.

There is a nuclear bomb somewhere along the coast of the state of Georgia, which has not yet been found after being dropped there in 1958.

• • •

It is widely believed that Thomas Jefferson had at least two children with his slave Sally Hemings.

• • •

Ancient Egyptians used slabs of stone as pillows.

• • •

The body of England's King Richard III was found under a parking lot in 2013.

In 1931, China banned the book Alice in Wonderland because 'animals should not use human language'.

• • •

In Ancient Rome, it was normal for 20-40% of children to be left outside to die of exposure.

• • •

Neil Armstrong and his Apollo 11 colleagues had to go through US Customs when they landed back on Earth from the moon.

• • •

One out of every 250 US citizens worked on the Manhattan Project during the Second World War.

Engineers have said that the Leaning Tower of Pisa has actually straightened by 1.5 inches since 2001.

• • •

Canaries were once used by miners as gas detectors.

• • •

George Washington almost didn't marry Martha — he was in love with his best friend's wife, Sally Fairfax.

• • •

Princeton researchers successfully turned a live cat into a functioning telephone in 1929.

Officially, the longest war in history was between the Netherlands and the Isles of Scilly. It lasted from 1651-1986. There were no casualties.

• • •

The reason why perfumes are sold at the front of department stores was to stop the smell of horse manure wafting into the store, back before shoppers had automobiles. It was first thought up by Harry Gordon Selfridge, founder of London's famous department store of the same name.

• • •

The phrase "Goodnight, sleep tight" originates from Shakespeare's time when mattresses were secured to bed frames by ropes. If you pulled on the ropes, the bed would tighten and become firmer to sleep on.

In 1912, a Paris orphanage held a raffle to raise money—the prizes were live babies.

• • •

England's King George I was born in Germany.

• • •

The very first bomb dropped by the Allies on Berlin during World War II had only one casualty — an elephant in the Berlin Zoo.

• • •

The metal rivets on your jeans aren't just for show — they were originally used to protect your jeans from tearing at weak spots. This was particularly important as they were mostly used by the working class population.

The first law dictating minimum wage requirements in the US was instituted in 1938. The minimum hourly wage was 25 cents.

• • •

Written language was invented independently by the Egyptians, Sumerians, Chinese, and Mayans.

• • •

The Nazis put a $5,000 bounty on Einstein's head.

• • •

Thomas Jefferson — an avid reader – sold over 6,000 books to the government, which formed the basis of the Library of Congress.

The shortest war on record was the Anglo-Zanzibar war, which lasted a whopping 38 minutes.

• • •

Tom Hanks is a third cousin, four generations removed, of Abraham Lincoln.

• • •

The word 'music' comes from the muses, Greek goddesses of the arts.

• • •

Tiffany's, the luxury jewelry store, was founded before Italy was even a country.

Ota Benga, a 23-year-old boy from Congo was exhibited in the Bronx zoo, New York, in a monkey house.

• • •

Vincent Van Gogh painted "The Starry Night" shortly after checking into a psychiatric hospital in 1889.

• • •

'Mountain Dew' was once a slang term for moonshine (homemade whiskey) in the south of the US and parts of the UK.

• • •

The Hershey chocolate bar was used as currency overseas during World War II.

During prohibition, Al Capone made $60 million a year from selling alcohol.

• • •

The Great Pyramid of Giza has eight sides, not four.

• • •

The guillotine was still used in France right up until 1977 — the same year that the first Star Wars movie came out.

• • •

In the 1880's, cocaine was sold as a medicine to cure sore throats, headaches, colds and sleeplessness.

The swastika was originally a symbol of peace and honor. It is still used today by Buddhists, particularly in Nepal.

• • •

The Bank of America was originally called the Bank of Italy.

• • •

In 1906, a man named Joe Munch was sentenced to one minute in jail.

• • •

The oldest condoms ever found date back to the 1640's; they were made from fish and animal intestines and found in Birmingham, England.

Albert Einstein acquired citizenship for five different countries: USA, Germany, Austria, Switzerland and Kingdom of Württemberg.

• • •

Despite popular belief, Viking helmets did not have horns on them — in fact, only one helmet from that era has been found with horns on it.

• • •

Buzz Aldrin was the first man to pee on the moon — he did so shortly after stepping off the spacecraft.

• • •

John Tyler — the 10th President of the United States — still has two grandsons that are alive.

Harvard University was founded before Calculus was discovered.

• • •

In 1971, astronaut Al Shepard played golf on the moon.

• • •

During World War II, a spy named Joan Pujol Garcia received the highest honor from both the Axis and the Allies — a testament to his double agent skills.

• • •

Before he became pope, Pius II wrote a best-selling erotic book: The Tale of Two Lovers.

The most common sacrifice of the Mayans was a beating heart pulled from a victim's chest.

• • •

The current version of the United States flag was designed by a high school student, who initially got a B- for his design. However, the student went back to his teacher after the flag was adopted by the government, and his grade was changed to an A.

• • •

When Concorde was still flying, it was possible to get to New York from London earlier than you left.

• • •

The longest ever space walk lasted around nine hours.

If you point a laser at an aircraft in the USA you could go to prison for 20 years.

• • •

In 2008, Guatemala became the first country to recognize femicide — the murder of a woman due to her gender — as a crime.

• • •

A conman by the name of Victor Lustig managed to sell the Eiffel Tower twice. He was later caught after he fled to the USA.

• • •

In 1567, a man who was said to have the world's longest beard died after tripping over said beard while trying to escape a fire.

There is a single common ancestor behind blue eyes.

• • •

The 'Pinky Promise' originally meant that if anyone broke a promise they would have to cut their pinky finger off.

• • •

After the 1066 Conquest, French was the official language of England for over 300 years.

• • •

In 2007, a man by the name of Corey Taylor tried to fake his own death to get out of a phone contract. He failed.

When the first of the Egyptian pyramids was built, woolly mammoths still walked the Earth.

• • •

Since 1970, the National Library Service for the Blind and Physically Handicapped has been publishing Braille versions of Playboy magazine; it does not include the pictures.

• • •

In the 1920's, radioactive Radium featured in many consumer products including toothpaste, cosmetics and even condoms.

• • •

The wristwatch was invented in 1904.

In the 1860's, the entire central city of Chicago was raised by several feet to fix a sewage problem — and everyone just carried on their business without noticing.

• • •

The $ sign was introduced in the late 1700's.

• • •

Popcorn was discovered as an accident by the Aztec Indians.

• • •

Neil Armstrong first stepped on the moon with his left foot.

Christopher Columbus brought cacao (chocolate) beans back to Spain in 1502 — his fourth voyage.

• • •

The Ancient Egyptian word for 'cat' was pronounced 'miw'.

• • •

The time difference between Stegosaurus and Tyrannosaurus Rex is greater than the time difference between Tyrannosaurus Rex and the first humans.

• • •

In ancient Greece, throwing an apple to a girl was a way to propose marriage. If she caught the apple, that meant she accepted.

In ancient Athens, if a jury found you guilty of sleeping with another man's wife, the man whose wife you slept with had the right to sodomize you with a radish.

• • •

Leonardo Da Vinci could write with one hand and draw with the other at the same time.

• • •

In the Ice Age, the British would use skulls of the dead as cups.

• • •

Native Americans used pumpkin seeds for both food and medicine.

Hawaii officially became a state of the United States on August 21, 1959.

• • •

In 1836, Mexican General Santa Anna had an expensive state funeral for his amputated leg.

• • •

The last man on the moon, Gene Cernan, promised his daughter he'd write her initials on the moon. He did, and they will probably be there for tens of thousands of years.

• • •

Before the mid-19th century, dentures were often made from teeth pulled from dead soldiers.

Seatbelts became mandatory in cars in the USA on March 1, 1968.

• • •

Trained pigeons would deliver secret messages over enemy lines during war time.

• • •

The first ever television remote was called "Lazy Bones".

• • •

In ancient Egypt, Pharaohs would smear their servants with honey so that they would attract the flies.

The propulsion system used on subway trains was derived from the technology used in elevators.

• • •

Around 50 per cent of all U.S. Presidents have been left-handed.

• • •

At President Andrew Jackson's funeral in 1845, his pet parrot was removed for swearing.

• • •

In early Rome, it was legal for a father to kill any member of his family.

In the 19th Century there was a popular cough medicine for kids called 'Mrs Winslow's Soothing Syrup', which contained morphine.

• • •

In medieval times, animals were often put on trial and many were sent to death.

• • •

The first passengers on a hot air balloon were a sheep, a duck and a rooster.

• • •

February 1865 was the only month in recorded history that didn't have a full moon.

In 16th Century Canada, women would drink ground beaver testicles as a contraceptive method.

• • •

Thomas Jefferson was the first U.S. President to be inaugurated in Washington D.C.

Sources

1. *For 50 Years, Nuclear Bomb Lost in Watery Grave* https://www.npr.org/templates/story/story.php?storyId=18587608

2. *Thomas Jefferson and Sally Hemings: A Brief Account* https://www.monticello.org/thomas-jefferson/jefferson-slavery/thomas-jefferson-and-sally-hemings-a-brief-account/

3. *Why Did Ancient Egyptians Use Pillows Made Of Stone?* http://www.ancientpages.com/2018/06/18/why-did-ancient-egyptians-use-pillows-made-of-stone/

4. *Body found under parking lot is King Richard III, scientists prove* https://edition.cnn.com/2013/02/03/world/europe/richard-iii-search-announcement/index.html

5. *Raising Kids Isn't Easy. Parenting Advice Often Makes It Harder.* https://www.nytimes.com/2019/01/02/books/review-act-natural-cultural-history-parenting-jennifer-traig.html

6. *Alice in Wonderland was a Banned Book but for a Weird Reason* https://www.ripleys.com/weird-news/alice-wonderland-banned-book/

7. *Back from the Moon, Apollo Astronauts Had to Go Through Customs* https://www.space.com/7044-moon-apollo-astronauts-customs.html

8. *More About Our Profiles* https://www.atomicheritage.org/more-about-our-profiles

9. *Leaning Tower of Pisa straightening its posture* https://www.curbed.com/2018/11/27/18113558/leaning-tower-of-pisa-straightening

10. *Domestic canary* https://en.wikipedia.org/wiki/Domestic_canary

11. *The Alleged Amorous Affairs of Washington* https://allthingsliberty.com/2016/03/the-alleged-amorous-affairs-of-washington/

12. *The Cat Telephone | Mudd Manuscript Library Blog* https://blogs.princeton.edu/mudd/2017/04/the-cat-telephone/

13. *Longest War With Fewest Casualties* https://www.historychannel.com.au/articles/longest-war-with-fewest-casualties/

14. *Who started/popularized the department store perfume gauntlet?* https://history.stackexchange.com/questions/8370/who-started-popularized-the-department-store-perfume-gauntlet

15. *Canvassing the Masterpieces: The Starry Night by Vincent van Gogh* https://www.kazoart.com/blog/en/canvassing-the-masterpieces-the-starry-night-by-vincent-van-gogh/

16. *Visiting Selfridges department store in London* https://kasiawrites.com/selfridges-department-store/

17. *Here's Why People Say 'Don't Let The Bedbugs Bite'* https://www.huffpost.com/en-

try/heres-why-people-say-dont-let-the-bedbugs-bite_n_5a5eb9e6e4b00a7f171b947c

18. *The 1911 Baby Raffle in Paris: Why It Matters* https://time.com/4433717/paris-baby-raffle-history/

19. *George I of Great Britain* https://en.wikipedia.org/wiki/George_I_of_Great_Britain

20. *The First Bomb Dropped by The Allies on Berlin Didn't Harm Anyone But Did Hit an Elephant in Berlin Zoo!* https://www.warhistoryonline.com/instant-articles/the-first-bomb-the-allies.html

21. *Those tiny bits of metal on the pockets of your jeans are actually really important* https://www.independent.co.uk/life-style/fashion/those-tiny-bits-of-metal-on-your-jeans-pockets-are-actually-really-important-a6998821.html

22. *Fair Labor Standards Act of 1938: Maximum Struggle for a Minimum Wage* https://www.dol.gov/general/aboutdol/history/flsa1938

23. *Where did writing begin?* https://www.bl.uk/history-of-writing/articles/where-did-writing-begin

24. *Albert Einstein* https://en.wikipedia.org/wiki/Albert_Einstein

25. *Jefferson's Library - Thomas Jefferson | Exhibitions* https://www.loc.gov/exhibits/jefferson/jefflib.html

26. *Anglo-Zanzibar War* https://en.wikipedia.org/wiki/Anglo-Zanzibar_War

27. *Nancy Lincoln* https://en.wikipedia.org/wiki/Nancy_Lincoln

28. *MUSES (Mousai) - Greek Goddesses of Music, Poetry & the Arts* https://www.theoi.com/Ouranios/Mousai.html

29. *Tiffany & Co. : when and how was it founded?* https://theeyeofjewelry.com/tiffany-co/tiffany-co-news/tiffany-co-when-and-how-was-it-founded/

30. *Ota Benga* https://en.wikipedia.org/wiki/Ota_Benga

31. *Mountain Dew* https://en.wikipedia.org/wiki/Mountain_Dew

32. *Joey Hacks* http://www.wackyuses.com/weirdfacts/hershey.html

33. *The Speakeasies of the 1920s* http://prohibition.themobmuseum.org/the-history/the-prohibition-underworld/the-speakeasies-of-the-1920s/

34. *The Eight Faces Of The Great Pyramid Of Giza* https://curiosity.com/topics/the-eight-faces-of-the-great-pyramid-of-giza-curiosity/

35. *Guillotine* https://en.wikipedia.org/wiki/Guillotine

36. *7 of the Most Outrageous Medical Treatments in History* https://www.history.com/news/7-of-the-most-outrageous-medical-treatments-in-history

37. *Swastika* https://en.wikipedia.org/wiki/Swastika

38. *1906 article in the Los Angeles Herald* https://cdnc.ucr.edu/?a=d&d=LAH19060312.2.44&e=-------en--20--1--txt-txIN--------1

39. *Birth Control History on MedicineNet.com* https://www.medicinenet.com/script/main/art.asp?articlekey=52188

40. *Einstein Archive* https://artsandculture.google.com/exhibit/albert-einstein-german-swiss-and-american-%C2%A0-%C2%A0-einstein-archive/QQrk18h6?hl=en

41. *Did Vikings really wear horned helmets?* https://www.history.com/news/did-vikings-really-wear-horned-helmets

42. *Buzz Aldrin* https://en.wikipedia.org/wiki/Buzz_Aldrin

43. *President John Tyler's Grandsons Are Still Alive* https://www.mentalfloss.com/article/29842/president-john-tylers-grandsons-are-still-alive

44. *Which Came First: Harvard or Calculus?* https://harvardx.harvard.edu/blog/which-came-first-harvard-university-or-calculus

45. *Today in golf: Alan Shepard plays golf on the moon* https://www.golf.com/extra-spin/2017/02/06/today-golf-alan-shepard-plays-golf-moon

46. *Juan Pujol García* https://en.wikipedia.org/wiki/Juan_Pujol_Garc%C3%ADa#Honours

47. *The Tale of Two Lovers* https://en.wikipedia.org/wiki/The_Tale_of_Two_Lovers

48. *Human sacrifice in Maya culture* https://en.wikipedia.org/wiki/Human_sacrifice_in_Maya_culture#Heart_removal

49. *How a High Schooler Designed the Current American Flag* https://www.rd.com/true-stories/inspiring/american-flag-high-school-project/

50. *Concorde* https://en.wikipedia.org/wiki/Concorde

51. *List of longest spacewalks* https://en.wikipedia.org/wiki/List_of_longest_spacewalks

52. *The FBI Would Like Everyone To Stop Shooting Lasers at Airplanes* https://www.smithsonianmag.com/smart-news/the-fbi-would-like-everyone-to-stop-shooting-lasers-at-airplanes-65075392/

53. *Femicide* https://apps.who.int/iris/bitstream/handle/10665/77421/WHO_RHR_12.38_eng.pdf?sequence=1

54. *Victor Lustig* https://en.wikipedia.org/wiki/Victor_Lustig

55. *8. Death by Beard - 10 Bizarre Ways to Die | HowStuffWorks* https://health.howstuffworks.com/diseases-conditions/death-dying/10-ways-to-die3.htm

56. *Blue-eyed humans have a single, common ancestor* https://www.sciencedaily.com/releases/2008/01/080130170343.htm

57. *What Is the True Meaning Behind a "Pinky Promise"?* https://www.hercampus.com/school/tulane/what-true-meaning-behind-pinky-promise

58. *The Norman Conquest* https://www.bl.uk/learning/langlit/changlang/activities/lang/norman/normaninvasion.html

59. *Verizon Customer Faked Death to Escape Contract* https://www.wired.

com/2007/08/verizon-custome/

60. *Did Woolly Mammoths Still Roam Parts Of Earth When The Great Pyramids Were Built?* https://www.worldatlas.com/articles/did-woolly-mammoths-still-roam-parts-of-earth-when-the-great-pyramids-were-built.html

61. *For years, there was Playboy for blind people, then a Republican congressman tried to kill it* https://timeline.com/playboy-braille-blind-congress-ebd9cbc6d8e0

62. *Radium Historical Items Catalog - Final Report.* https://www.nrc.gov/docs/ML1008/ML100840118.pdf

63. *Raising of Chicago* https://en.wikipedia.org/wiki/Raising_of_Chicago

64. *Where did the dollar sign come from?* https://www.history.com/news/where-did-the-dollar-sign-come-from

65. *History of watches* https://en.wikipedia.org/wiki/History_of_watches

66. *Popcorn Board > Facts & Fun > History of Popcorn > Early Popcorn History* https://www.popcorn.org/Facts-Fun/History-of-Popcorn/Early-History-of-Popcorn

67. *Apollo 11 -- First Footprint on the Moon* https://www.nasa.gov/audience/forstudents/k-4/home/F_Apollo_11.html

68. *Discovering Chocolate* https://www.cadbury.com.au/About-Chocolate/Discovering-Chocolate.aspx

69. *"Meow" is just another name for "cat"* https://www.originofalphabet.com/meow-is-just-another-name-for-cat/

70. *The Stegosaurus Was An Ancient Relic To The T. Rex* https://curiosity.com/topics/the-stegosaurus-was-an-ancient-relic-to-the-t-rex-curiosity/

71. *In ancient Greece, throwing an apple at someone was considered a marriage proposal* https://www.thevintagenews.com/2016/09/10/ancient-greece-throwing-apple-someone-considered-marriage-proposal/

72. *What are some unusual facts about the ancient Greeks?* https://www.quora.com/What-are-some-unusual-facts-about-the-ancient-Greeks

73. *Leonardo Da Vinci 'could write, draw and paint with both hands', experts claim* https://www.independent.co.uk/arts-entertainment/art/news/leonardo-da-vinci-drawing-painting-write-ambidextrous-both-hands-italy-a8865611.html

74. *Ice age Britons ate each other and made cups from skulls* https://www.telegraph.co.uk/news/earth/environment/archaeology/8326115/Ice-age-Britons-ate-each-other-and-made-cups-from-skulls.html

75. *Pumpkin - Uses* https://wa.kaiserpermanente.org/kbase/topic.jhtml?docId=hn-2151005

76. *Hawaii Becomes our 50th State* http://www.americaslibrary.gov/jb/modern/jb_modern_hawaii_1.html

77. *History Meet the Mexican General Who Gave His Leg a Full State Burial* https://theculturetrip.com/north-america/mexico/articles/meet-the-mexican-general-who-gave-his-leg-a-full-state-burial/

78. *Eugene Cernan: Last Man on the Moon* https://www.space.com/20790-eugene-cer-

nan-astronaut-biography.html

79. *The dentures made from the teeth of dead soldiers at Waterloo* https://www.bbc.com/news/magazine-33085031

80. *Seat belt laws in the United States* https://en.wikipedia.org/wiki/Seat_belt_laws_in_the_United_States

81. *War pigeon* https://en.wikipedia.org/wiki/War_pigeon

82. *A history of the TV remote control as told through its advertising* https://www.metv.com/stories/a-history-of-the-television-remote-control-as-told-through-its-advertising

83. *Pharoah Pepi II – Flies and Honey* http://www.creatinghistory.com/pharoah-pepi-ii-flies-and-honey/

84. *Electromagnetic propulsion* https://en.wikipedia.org/wiki/Electromagnetic_propulsion

85. *How many US presidents were left-handed?* https://www.govtech.com/question-of-the-day/Question-of-the-Day-for-02172015.html

86. *Andrew Jackson's Funeral* https://eu.tennessean.com/story/news/2015/06/07/andrew-jacksons-funeral-drew-thousands-swearing-parrot/28664493/

87. *Pater familias* https://en.wikipedia.org/wiki/Pater_familias

88. *MRS. WINSLOW'S SOOTHING SYRUP FOR CHILDREN TEETHING.; LETTER FROM A MOTHER IN LOWELL, MASS. A DOWN-TOWN MERCHANT.* https://www.nytimes.com/1860/12/01/archives/mrs-winslows-soothing-syrup-for-children-teething-letter-from-a.html

89. *Fantastically Wrong: Europe's Insane History of Putting Animals on Trial and Executing Them* https://www.wired.com/2014/09/fantastically-wrong-europes-insane-history-putting-animals-trial-executing/

89. *The fabulous story of the first hot air balloon flights - Aleph* https://www.faena.com/aleph/articles/the-fabulous-story-of-the-first-hot-air-balloon-flights/

90. *What year and month did not have a full moon* https://www.answers.com/Q/What_year_and_month_did_not_have_a_full_moon

91. *World Contraception Day: 10 of history's most horrible contraceptives* https://www.bbc.co.uk/bbcthree/article/e671cb02-4e5e-4f52-a835-25a5dd2a5963

92. *List of United States presidential firsts* https://en.wikipedia.org/wiki/List_of_United_States_presidential_firsts

Music
& Entertainment

Music and entertainment make the world a better place, right?! Whether you love dancing to Billie Eilish's latest hit or staying up-to-date on Taylor Swift's love life, there's no denying it's a huge part of our lives.

We've uncovered some fascinating facts about our favorite musicians and celebrities. Enjoy!

Al Gore and Tommy Lee Jones were freshman roommates at Harvard University.

• • •

Woody Allen's real name is Allen Stewart Konigsberg.

• • •

Jake Gyllenhaal's first driving lesson was from Paul Newman, who was a close family friend.

• • •

George Clooney slept in a friend's closet for a year when he first moved to LA.

Your heartbeat changes depending on the music you're listening to.

• • •

In the music industry, for every $1,000 of music sold, the average musician gets $23.40.

• • •

The Beatles officially broke up at Disney World.

• • •

Charlize Theron was "discovered" when an agent witnessed her throwing a fit at a bank teller who wouldn't cash her check.

Russell Brand was legally entitled to take $20 million from Katy Perry's fortune when they divorced, but refused to take any.

• • •

The movie Paranormal Activity cost $15000 to make and grossed $210 million.

• • •

To thank Robin Williams for his work on *Aladdin*, and to settle a dispute they had between them, Disney sent him a late Pablo Picasso painting worth $1 million.

• • •

Harry Styles from *One Direction* has two extra nipples.

Ryan Gosling was cast as Noah in *The Notebook* because the director wanted someone "not handsome."

• • •

Brad Pitt's first job was as a chicken mascot at a fast food restaurant.

• • •

Elton John is Eminen's A.A. sponsor.

• • •

Lisa Kudrow was originally cast as Roz in *Frasier*, but was fired before it aired.

Jon Cryer, from *Two and a Half Men*, was offered the role of Chandler in *Friends*, but turned it down. Sarah Jessica Parker was the only actor in *Sex and the City* to have a no nudity clause in her contract.

• • •

Cynthia Nixon is a natural blonde, so had to dye her hair red for her role in *Sex and the City*.

• • •

The *Desperate Housewives* set was previously used in Kelly Rowland and Nelly's video for "*Dilemma*".

• • •

Emilia Clarke, who plays Daenerys in *Game of Thrones*, voiced Dr. Zoidberg's girlfriend in the final episodes of *Futurama*.

Selma Blair and Katie Holmes were in the running to play Buffy in *Buffy the Vampire Slayer*.

• • •

Shakira was rejected from her school's choir because they thought she sounded like a goat.

• • •

Americans cast more votes in the voting of Taylor Hicks in *American Idol* than the 1984 presidential election of Ronald Reagan.

• • •

Madonna suffers from brontophobia aka astraphobia — a fear of thunderstorms.

Daniel Craig used to sleep on park benches when he was a struggling actor.

• • •

Oprah's birth name was 'Orpah', named after the sister of Ruth in the Bible. She changed it because so many people got it wrong.

• • •

Alfred Hitchcock's *Psycho* (1960) was the first American film ever to show a flushing toilet.

• • •

Taylor Swift's first job was to knock praying mantises off Christmas trees at the farm her parents owned.

Bender from *Futurama* was named after John Bender from *The Breakfast Club*.

• • •

In *Saving Private Ryan* all of the main cast were given basic military training except Matt Damon, in the hope that the cast would build a resentment towards him necessary for the role.

• • •

Darth Vader only has 12 minutes of screen time in the original *Star Wars*.

• • •

The movie *Saw* was filmed in 18 days.

Pierce Brosnan was contractually forbidden from wearing a full tuxedo in any non-James Bond movie from 1995-2002.

• • •

The charcoal drawing of Kate Winslet in *Titanic* was drawn by James Cameron.

• • •

Many scenes in the movie *28 Days Later* were filmed on a Canon XL-1 DV camera using mini-DV tapes instead of 35mm film.

• • •

Daniel Radcliffe's stunt double was paralyzed during the last Harry Potter film, so he set up a fundraiser to pay for him to go to college.

E.T. and Poltergeist were originally meant to be one movie.

• • •

Beyonce has trained herself to be able to sing while running a mile, which helps prepare her for her high-energy concerts.

• • •

Sean Connery wore a wig in every James Bond film.

• • •

Elton John's real name is Reginald Dwight.

Barbie in *Toy Story 2* and 3 is voiced by Jodi Benson, best known for her role as Ariel in *The Little Mermaid*.

• • •

Actor John Hurt has died in more than 40 movies — a world record.

• • •

Beethoven began losing his hearing at the age of 28, so he cut the legs off of his piano so he could compose music by feeling the vibrations of the piano on the floor.

• • •

It cost more to make the movie Titanic than it did to build the original ship.

The cartoon Pokemon's flashing graphics sent 618 Japanese children to hospital with seizures and nausea during one episode.

• • •

Django Unchained was the first time in 16 years that Leonardo DiCaprio didn't get the top billing.

• • •

The sound of the velociraptors mating in Jurassic Park is actually the sound of tortoises mating.

• • •

Star Wars was originally prefixed with 'The'.

The chills you get when you listen to music is mostly caused by the brain releasing dopamine — a feel-good chemical — while anticipating the peak moment of a song.

• • •

Actor Tim Allen (Home Improvement, Buzz Lightyear) spent two years in prison for trafficking cocaine.

• • •

Ricky Martin's real name is Enrique Martín Morales.

• • •

The Partridge Family TV drummer Brian Forster is the great-great-great grandson of Charles Dickens.

Playing music regularly can alter your brain structure.

• • •

James Franco worked at McDonald's after dropping out of UCLA. He would practice his foreign accents on customers.

• • •

Robert De Niro dropped out of high school to head straight to acting school.

• • •

Jack Nicholson grew up thinking his grandmother was his mom and his mom his sister. He was born to his 'sister' when she was 17. He didn't find out until he was 37 and both of them had passed away.

Paul McCartney never learned to read music.

• • •

Johannes Brahms got his start playing piano in brothels.

• • •

The first CD to be pressed in the USA was Bruce Springsteen's Born in the USA.

• • •

The first cell phone was invented in 1924.

• • •

During the filming of *The Wolf of Wall Street*, Jonah Hill snorted so much fake cocaine that he got bronchitis.

Kate Bosworth has one blue eye and one hazel eye. The condition is known as heterochromia.

• • •

Rowan Atkinson (aka Mr Bean) is a qualified Electrical Engineer.

• • •

During the filming of X-Men, Hugh Jackman went through approximately 700 claws for his role as Wolverine.

• • •

On average, Americans spend over 11 hours a day consuming digital media.

Jean-Claude Van Damme was once homeless and lived on the streets of Los Angeles.

• • •

The most searched for tutorial video on Youtube is 'how to kiss'.

• • •

In 2019, Jennifer Aniston became the fastest person to reach 1 million followers on Instagram, in just 5 hours and 16 minutes.

• • •

Ashton Kutcher has a condition called syndactyly, meaning his toes are webbed together.

Robert De Niro saw the Twin Towers collapse from the window of his New York home.

• • •

"London Bridge is Down" is the broadcasting code for when the Queen passes away.

• • •

Betty White is older than sliced bread. That's right, sliced bread was introduced in 1928 and Betty White was born in 1922.

• • •

Jason Statham was on the British National Swimming squad for 12 years before becoming a Hollywood actor.

Matthew Perry is missing the top part of his right-hand middle finger after his grandfather trapped it in a door when he was young.

• • •

Brian May, the lead guitarist of Queen, has a PhD in Astrophysics.

• • •

A study has found that Snapchat provokes more jealousy in relationships than Facebook.

• • •

Supermodel Karolina Kurkova has no belly button. It was removed during an operation when she was younger.

Mortimer Mouse was the original name for Mickey Mouse. Walt Disney's wife was the one who convinced him to change it.

• • •

Seth Macfarlane, creator of *Family Guy*, had a ticket booked for one of the ill-fated 9/11 flights but missed it.

• • •

In the first Dumb & Dumber movie, Jeff Daniels made just $50,000, while Jim Carrey was paid $7 million.

While filming *I am Legend,* Will Smith got so attached to his German Shepherd co-star, that he asked if he could keep her, but the owner refused.

• • •

There's a hotline in Germany called 'Schimpf-Los' which means 'swear away'. People can call the number to let off steam after a stressful day.

• • •

Paul McCartney is the only musician to top the music charts as a solo artist, in a duo, trio, quartet and quintet.

• • •

Olympic gold medallist, George Foreman, has five sons who are all called George.

Facebook will accept 3 versions of your password: as it is; case inverted (in case you left caps lock on); and the password with the first letter capitalized (for mobile devices, which often automatically start with a capital).

• • •

Long before he became an actor/comedian, Ricky Gervais was part of the 80s glam pop duo Seona Dancing.

• • •

Elvis Presley was born blonde.

• • •

In 1967, the Beatles almost bought an island off the coast of Athens, Greece with the plans to build a utopian community.

Brad Pitt tore his Achilles tendon while playing the role of Achilles in the movie Troy.

• • •

Popeye's four nephews are called Pipeye, Peepeye, Pupeye and Poopeye.

• • •

In 2013, Mark Zuckerberg spent 30 million dollars buying four houses that surround his own home to ensure he had privacy.

• • •

The voice of Chris in *Family Guy* is based on Buffalo Bill from Silence of the Lambs.

Paul McCartney was once kicked out of Germany for lighting a condom on fire.

• • •

At the 2020 Grammy Awards, Billie Eilish became the youngest person ever to win the main four awards. Previously, Taylor Swift held the record.

Sources

1. *Tommy Lee Jones and Al Gore | 8 sets of famous college roommates | MNN* https://www.mnn.com/lifestyle/arts-culture/photos/8-sets-of-famous-college-roommates/tommy-lee-jones-and-al-gore
2. *Woody Allen* https://en.wikipedia.org/wiki/Woody_Allen
3. *15 Amazing Things We Never Knew About Jake Gyllenhaal* https://www.thethings.com/15-amazing-things-we-never-knew-about-jake-gyllenhaal/
4. *George Clooney News & Biography* https://www.empireonline.com/people/george-clooney/7/
5. *Heart Beat: Music May Help Keep Your Cardiovascular System in Tune* https://www.scientificamerican.com/article/music-therapy-heart-cardiovascular/
6. *RIAA Accounting: Why Even Major Label Musicians Rarely Make Money From Album Sales* https://www.techdirt.com/articles/20100712/23482610186.shtml
7. *John Lennon Officially Ended the Beatles at Disney World* https://ultimateclassicrock.com/john-lennon-ended-beatles-at-disney/
8. *Charlize Theron - Biography* https://www.imdb.com/name/nm0000234/bio
9. *Russell Brand says no to Katy Perry's $44 million fortune in 'amicable' divorce* https://www.news.com.au/entertainment/celebrity-life/russell-brand-says-no-to-katy-perrys-fortune-in-amicable-divorce/news-story/4f7a7300fb53743e88677f4d2b6f0b3b?sv=9fd886b2a4677ed165bc86c50a93451f
10. *Paranormal Activity* https://en.wikipedia.org/wiki/Paranormal_Activity
11. *Robin Williams Disney Feud Led To Picasso Gift* https://www.businessinsider.com/robin-williams-disney-feud-picasso-gift-2014-11?IR=T
12. *Harry Styles Confirms He Has Four Nipples, a Condition Called Polythelia* https://www.allure.com/story/harry-styles-confirms-he-has-four-nipples
13. *30+ Facts About 'The Notebook' Every Fan Needs to Know* https://www.womansday.com/life/entertainment/g24674622/notebook-movie-facts/
14. *Brad Pitt has 'no shame' about his job as an El Pollo Loco mascot before making it big in Hollywood: 'Man's gotta eat'* https://www.insider.com/brad-pitt-el-pollo-loco-mascot-ellen-show-video-2019-9
15. *Why Lisa Kudrow Was Fired From Frasier* https://screenrant.com/lisa-kudrow-fired-from-frasier-reasons/
16. *These celebrities almost played your favourite Friends!* https://celebrity.nine.com.au/latest/these-stars-almost-played-your-favourite-friends/157786d4-dbfb-4be6-9fa9-b0bf74c396c3

17. *Sarah Jessica Parker Explains Why She Has a No-Nudity Contract Clause | In-Style.com* https://www.instyle.com/news/sarah-jessica-parker-no-nudity-contract-clause

18. *Redhead celebrities that are naturally blonde* https://www.insider.com/red-hair-celebrities-that-are-naturally-blonde#deborah-ann-woll-first-hit-it-big-as-a-redhead-but-more-recently-shes-embraced-her-natural-blonde-tresses-8

19. *How Elton John helped other celebrities struggling with addiction* https://pagesix.com/2019/10/16/how-elton-john-helped-other-celebrities-struggling-with-addiction/

20. *Dilemma (song)* https://en.wikipedia.org/wiki/Dilemma_(song)

21. *Stench and Stenchibility* https://en.wikipedia.org/wiki/Stench_and_Stenchibility

22. *Buffy the Vampire Slayer* https://en.wikipedia.org/wiki/Buffy_the_Vampire_Slayer

23. *Shakira's teacher told her she had a bad voice and banned her from the school choir* https://www.businessinsider.com/shakira-banned-from-school-choir-2016-3?IR=T

24. *American Idol outvotes the president | Media* https://www.theguardian.com/media/2006/may/26/realitytv.usnews

25. *Madonna - Famous Fears and Phobias* http://www.zimbio.com/Famous+Fears+and+Phobias/articles/vq_H6VMOzuq/Madonna

26. *15 Rich And Famous People Who Were Once Homeless* https://www.businessinsider.in/careers/15-rich-and-famous-people-who-were-once-homeless/slidelist/40128079.cms

27. *Oprah Winfrey* https://en.wikipedia.org/wiki/Oprah_Winfrey

28. *14 Crazy Facts About 'Psycho'* https://www.mentalfloss.com/article/68248/14-crazy-facts-about-psycho

29. *10 Things You Didn't Know About Taylor Swift* https://tasteofcountry.com/10-things-you-didnt-know-about-taylor-swift-7/

30. *The Surprising Origins of TV Character Names* https://www.mentalfloss.com/article/57016/surprising-origins-tv-character-names

31. *Saving Private Ryan* https://en.wikipedia.org/wiki/Saving_Private_Ryan

32. *10 Classic Film Characters Who Didn't Have As Much Screen-Time As You Thought* https://whatculture.com/film/10-classic-film-characters-didnt-much-screen-time-thought

33. *Saw (2004 film)* https://en.wikipedia.org/wiki/Saw_(2004_film)

34. *James Bond: Was Pierce Brosnan 'banned' from doing THIS while playing 007?* https://www.express.co.uk/entertainment/films/1072418/James-Bond-Pierce-Brosnan-banned-suits-tuxedos-007

35. *Topless drawing of Kate Winslet in Titanic to sell for £10,000* https://www.telegraph.co.uk/culture/art/art-news/8421218/Topless-drawing-of-Kate-Winslet-in-Titanic-to-sell-for-10000.html

36. *28 Days Later* https://en.wikipedia.org/wiki/28_Days_Later

37. *Harry Potter stuntman David Holmes speaks of moment he was left paralysed in horror film accident* https://www.mirror.co.uk/news/real-life-stories/harry-potter-stuntman-david-holmes-3255214

38. ***ET vs. Poltergeist: Two sides of the same Spielberg coin?*** https://www.syfy.com/syfywire/et-vs-poltergeist-two-sides-same-spielberg-coin

39. ***Beyoncé sang her album while running*** https://www.insider.com/beyonce-training-secret-singing-while-running-2017-11

40. ***007 Sean Connery, wore a hairpiece in every Bond movie he was in*** https://www.thevintagenews.com/2017/04/29/sean-connery-wore-a-hairpiece-in-every-of-his-bond-performances/

41. ***Elton John*** https://en.wikipedia.org/wiki/Elton_John

42. ***Jodi Benson*** https://en.wikipedia.org/wiki/Jodi_Benson

43. ***John Hurt, the actor who died in 'so many spectacular ways'*** https://www.washingtonpost.com/news/arts-and-entertainment/wp/2017/01/28/hurtdeath/

44. ***"Ludwig van Beethoven"*** https://www.lifeprint.com/asl101/topics/beethoven02.htm

45. ***Titanic (1997) - Trivia*** https://www.imdb.com/title/tt0120338/trivia

46. ***Flashing Japan Cartoon Makes Children Sick*** https://www.latimes.com/archives/la-xpm-1997-dec-17-mn-64975-story.html

47. ***Django Unchained (2012) - Trivia*** https://www.imdb.com/title/tt1853728/trivia

48. ***The Raptor Noises in Jurassic Park Are Mating Tortoises*** https://www.sciencealert.com/the-raptor-noises-in-jurassic-park-are-mating-tortoises

49. ***Star Wars (film)*** https://en.wikipedia.org/wiki/Star_Wars_(film)

50. ***Musical chills: Why they give us thrills*** https://www.sciencedaily.com/releases/2011/01/110112111117.htm

51. ***Tim Allen*** https://en.wikipedia.org/wiki/Tim_Allen

52. ***Ricky Martin*** https://en.wikipedia.org/wiki/Ricky_Martin

53. ***Brian Forster*** https://en.wikipedia.org/wiki/Brian_Forster

54. ***Learning With Music Can Change Brain Structure*** https://neurosciencenews.com/music-learning-brain-structure-7037/

55. ***James Franco on Dropping Out of UCLA and Practicing Accents at McDonald's*** https://variety.com/2017/tv/news/james-franco-dustin-hoffman-actors-on-actors-1202628665/

56. ***Robert De Niro*** https://en.wikipedia.org/wiki/Robert_De_Niro

57. ***Jack Nicholson's Mother*** https://www.snopes.com/fact-check/you-dont-know-jack/

58. ***Paul McCartney admits he and the Beatles can't read or write music*** https://globalnews.ca/news/4503916/paul-mccartney-cant-read-music/

59. ***Did the Young Brahms Play Piano in Waterfront Bars?*** https://www.jstor.org/stable/10.1525/ncm.2001.24.3.268?seq=1

60. ***9/1984 The First Music CDs Pressed in the United States*** http://www.historyofinformation.com/detail.php?entryid=3541

61. ***The History Behind the Invention of the First Cell Phone*** https://interestingengi-

neering.com/the-history-behind-the-invention-of-the-first-cell-phone

62. *Jonah Hill ended up in hospital after snorting too much fake cocaine for Wolf of Wall Street* https://www.independent.co.uk/news/people/jonah-hill-fake-cocaine-wolf-of-wall-street-a7200886.html

63. *Heterochromia: 2 different colored eyes* https://www.allaboutvision.com/conditions/heterochromia.htm

64. *Rowan Atkinson* https://en.wikipedia.org/wiki/Rowan_Atkinson

65. *5 Facts About Hugh Jackman's Role As Wolverine To Get You Ready For LOGAN* https://www.playbuzz.com/johnnybosshart10/5-facts-about-hugh-jackmans-role-as-wolverine-to-get-you-ready-for-logan

66. *Time Flies: U.S. Adults Now Spend Nearly Half a Day Interacting with Media* https://www.nielsen.com/us/en/insights/article/2018/time-flies-us-adults-now-spend-nearly-half-a-day-interacting-with-media/

67. *Jean-Claude Van Damme* https://en.wikipedia.org/wiki/Jean-Claude_Van_Damme

68. *YouTube Viewers Really Want To Learn How To Kiss* https://www.fastcompany.com/3046271/youtube-viewers-really-want-to-learn-how-to-kiss

69. *Friends star Jennifer Aniston claims record for fastest to reach one million Instagram followers* https://www.guinnessworldrecords.com/news/2019/10/friends-star-jennifer-aniston-claims-record-for-fastest-to-reach-one-million-inst-595437/

70. *Webbed toes* https://en.wikipedia.org/wiki/Webbed_toes

71. *Robert De Niro, Martin Scorsese Reflect on the Birth of the Tribeca Film Festival* https://www.hollywoodreporter.com/news/tribeca-de-niro-martin-scorsese-181208

72. *Betty White is older than sliced bread.* https://www.justapinch.com/groups/discuss/205417/betty-white-is-older-than-sliced-bread

73. *Jason Statham* https://en.wikipedia.org/wiki/Jason_Statham

74. *Matthew Perry Is Missing The Tip Of His Finger And An Eagle-Eyed 'Friends' Viewer Finally Noticed* https://ruinmyweek.com/entertainment/matthew-perry-finger-friends/

75. *Brian May* https://en.wikipedia.org/wiki/Brian_May

76. *Snapchat is worse for your relationship than Facebook* https://www.thejournal.ie/snapchat-facebook-jealousy-2018616-Mar2015/

77. *Karolina Kurkova's Missing Bellybutton Explained (PHOTOS)* https://www.huffpost.com/entry/karolina-kurkovas-missing_n_145684

78. *Mickey Mouse* https://en.wikipedia.org/wiki/Mickey_Mouse

79. *Seth MacFarlane, The Brains Behind 'Family Guy', Missed One Of The Doomed 9/11 Flights* https://www.ladbible.com/more/interesting-creator-of-family-guy-missed-one-of-the-doomed-911-flights-20160527

80. *Farrelly Brothers Reveal Jim Carrey Made 7 Million* https://www.yahoo.com/entertainment/farrelly-brothers-reveal-jim-carrey-made-7-million-for-102378340427.html

81. *Will Smith falls in love with 'Legend' co-star* https://www.today.com/popculture/will-smith-falls-love-legend-co-star-wbna22264942

82. *Germans blow off steam with swearing hotline* https://www.reuters.com/article/us-germany-hotline/germans-blow-off-steam-with-swearing-hotline-idUSBRE86O15420120725

83. *Pipes of Peace (song)* https://en.wikipedia.org/wiki/Pipes_of_Peace_(song)

84. *George Foreman* https://en.wikipedia.org/wiki/George_Foreman

85. *Facebook passwords are not case sensitive (update)* https://www.zdnet.com/article/facebook-passwords-are-not-case-sensitive-update/

86. *Seona Dancing* https://en.wikipedia.org/wiki/Seona_Dancing

87. *Old Photo Proves Elvis Presley Was Actually Blonde* https://countrymusicnation.com/old-photo-proves-elvis-presley-was-actually-blonde

88. *The Beatles visit a Greek island they intended to purchase* https://www.beatlesbible.com/1967/07/26/beatles-visit-greek-island/

89. *Brad Pitt goes to extremes in 'Troy'* https://www.today.com/popculture/brad-pitt-goes-extremes-troy-wbna4953083

90. *Pipeye, Peepeye, Poopeye and Pupeye* https://popeye.fandom.com/wiki/Pipeye,_Peepeye,_Poopeye_and_Pupeye

91. *Mark Zuckerberg Buys 4 homes for privacy* https://www.businessinsider.com/mark-zuckerberg-buys-4-homes-for-privacy-2013-10?IR=T

92. *Stew-Roids* https://en.wikipedia.org/wiki/Stew-Roids

93. *Paul McCartney and Pete Best are arrested in Hamburg* https://www.beatlesbible.com/1960/11/29/paul-mccartney-pete-best-arrested-hamburg/

94. *Billie Eilish is the big winner at the Grammys* https://www.bbc.com/news/entertainment-arts-51260559

Literature & Language

Even with the growth of the internet and television, there will always be a place for a good book — or three — in our lives. Learn some amazing facts about some of your favorite books and authors. We've also thrown in a few interesting facts about foreign languages.

'Dreamt' is the only word in the English language that ends in the letters 'mt'.

• • •

Dr Seuss wrote Green Eggs and Ham as a bet against his publisher who said he couldn't write a book with only 50 words.

• • •

There was an outbreak of head lice among the cast of Harry Potter and the Chamber of Secrets.

• • •

Emily Brontë once had to put out her brother, Branwell, when he set fire to his bedclothes.

Before settling on his pen name of Mark Twain, Samuel Langhorne Clemens signed his writings with the pseudonym 'Josh'.

• • •

Various publishers rejected Harry Potter before Bloomsbury took it and published it.

• • •

People who read are two and a half times less likely to be diagnosed with Alzheimer's.

• • •

More than 750 million adults around the world cannot read or write.

The record for most people balancing books on their heads at the same place and time is 998 in Sydney, Australia, in 2012.

• • •

Reading fiction books has been proven to improve empathy.

• • •

The first novel written on a typewriter was Mark Twain's Adventures Of Tom Sawyer.

• • •

Shakespeare was also an actor, and performed in many of his plays.

74% of Americans said they read at least one book per year.

• • •

William Shakespeare is credited to have contributed over 2,000 new words to the existing English Dictionary we all use today.

• • •

J.K. Rowling is the only person on the Forbes rich list whose source of wealth is 'selling novels'.

• • •

Harper Lee initially threw her book *To Kill a Mockingbird* out of his window into the snow. It hasn't been out of print since it was published over 70 years ago.

Before the book *Peter Pan* was written, the name Wendy was considered to be a man's name. Later, it became a popular girl's name.

• • •

The world's most expensive book ever purchased was bought by Bill Gates for $30.8 million. It was Codex Leicester by Leonardo Da Vinci.

• • •

Dr Seuss included the word 'contraceptive' in a draft of his children's book Hop on Pop to make sure his publisher was paying attention.

• • •

The earliest recorded use of 'wicked' to mean 'cool, good' is from F. Scott Fitzgerald's first novel, *This Side of Paradise.*

As a schoolboy in England, Roald Dahl was a taste-tester for Cadbury's chocolate.

• • •

Sting wrote the song *Every Breath You Take* at the same desk which Ian Fleming used to write his James Bond novels. It was at the 'Fleming Villa' in Jamaica.

• • •

In 1871, Mark Twain invented one of the first bra clasps.

• • •

People in India are the world's biggest readers, spending an average 10.7 hours a week.

J. K. Rowling came up with the names for the houses at Hogwarts in Harry Potter while she was on a plane. She jotted the names down on a sick-bag.

• • •

The best-selling non-fiction book of all time that has reliable sales figures is *The Lord of the Rings*.

• • •

Charles Dickens believed in ghosts and he belonged to *The Ghost Club*.

• • •

The original manuscript of John Steinbeck's *Of Mice and Men* was eaten by his dog, Toby.

One of William Shakespeare's relatives on his mother's side, William Arden, was arrested for plotting against Queen Elizabeth I, imprisoned in the Tower of London and executed.

• • •

To Kill a Mockingbird was Harper Lee's only novel until *Go Set a Watchman,* which was an early draft of To Kill a Mockingbird, was published in 2015.

• • •

The original version of Roald Dahl's Charlie and the Chocolate Factory had several racist references; it has since been edited.

• • •

Pride and Prejudice was originally called *First Impressions.*

Poet Samuel Taylor Coleridge joined the army under the name Silas Tomkyn Cumberbatch.

• • •

Many English words come from the Dutch, including yacht, easel, cookie and freight.

• • •

Epäjärjestelmällistyttämättömyydellänsäkäänköhä is the longest word in the Finnish language. It means 'doubtful'.

• • •

There are over 300 languages spoken in London.

• • •

The Lithuanian language has many similarities to sanskrit.

There are at least 20 countries around the world that have only one person left who can speak it.

• • •

The average native English speaker (aged 20) knows around 42,000 words.

• • •

Studies have shown that speaking a second language can help prevent dementia.

• • •

Papua New Guinea has 851 langauges.

Sources

1. *Which English Words End With -mt?* https://www.lexico.com/explore/words-ending-with-mt

2. *Green Eggs and Ham* https://en.wikipedia.org/wiki/Green_Eggs_and_Ham

3. *15 Behind-The-Scenes Drama You Didn't Know About 'Harry Potter'* https://www.thethings.com/15-behind-the-scenes-drama-you-didnt-know-about-harry-potter/

4. *Five Fascinating Facts about the Brontë Sisters* https://interestingliterature.com/2014/04/five-fascinating-facts-about-the-bronte-sisters/

5. *Mark Twain* https://en.wikipedia.org/wiki/Mark_Twain

6. *This Is The 'Harry Potter' Synopsis Publishers Rejected Over 20 Years Ago* https://www.huffpost.com/entry/harry-potter-synopsis-jk-rowling_n_59f1e294e4b043885915a95c

7. *Reading, Chess May Help Fight Alzheimer's* https://abcnews.go.com/Health/story?id=117588&page=1

8. *750 million adults around the world cannot read a story like this one* https://theirworld.org/news/750-million-adults-around-the-world-cannot-read-a-story-like-this-one

9. *Most people balancing books on their heads* https://www.guinnessworldrecords.com/world-records/most-people-balancing-books-on-their-heads/

10. *Does reading fiction make us better people?* https://www.bbc.com/future/article/20190523-does-reading-fiction-make-us-better-people

11. *Mark Twain Wrote the First Book Ever Written With a Typewriter* http://www.openculture.com/2013/03/mark_twain_wrote_the_first_book_ever_written_with_a_typewriter.html

12. *Did Shakespeare act in any of his plays and if so, what roles did he perform?* https://www.enotes.com/homework-help/did-shakespeare-act-any-his-plays-what-roles-did-452575

13. *This Is How Many Books The Average American Reads In A Year* https://www.bustle.com/p/how-many-books-did-the-average-american-read-in-the-last-year-this-new-study-may-surprise-you-8837851

14. *Vocabulary* https://en.wikipedia.org/wiki/Shakespeare%27s_influence#Vocabulary

15. *JK Rowling* https://www.forbes.com/profile/jk-rowling/#2092048e3aeb

16. *Harper Lee* https://en.wikipedia.org/wiki/Harper_Lee

17. *Wendy* https://en.wikipedia.org/wiki/Wendy

18. *Look inside the Codex Leicester, which Bill Gates bought for $30 million* https://www.businessinsider.com/look-inside-the-codex-leicester-which-bill-gates-bought-for-30-million-2015-7?IR=T

19. *Five Fascinating Facts about Dr Seuss* https://interestingliterature.com/2015/03/five-fascinating-facts-about-dr-seuss/

20. *F. Scott Fitzgerald Adds to the Oxford English Dictionary* https://newsfeed.time.com/2013/05/08/why-f-scott-fitzgerald-is-all-over-the-dictionary/

21. *The Inventing Room* https://www.roalddahl.com/roald-dahl/archive/archive-highlights/the-inventing-room

22. *Visit the home of James Bond, Ian Fleming's Goldeneye estate* https://www.mi6-hq.com/sections/articles/style_goldeneye_visit.php3

23. *Mark Twain Invented the Bra Clasp* https://curiosity.com/topics/mark-twain-invented-the-bra-clasp-curiosity/

24. *DATA STORY: Indians spend more time reading than anyone else in the world* https://www.moneycontrol.com/news/trends/data-story-indians-spend-more-time-reading-than-anyone-else-in-the-world-2425835.html

25. *J.K. Rowling Wrote One Of The Most Important Parts Of Harry Potter On An Airplane Vomit Bag* https://www.bustle.com/p/jk-rowling-reveals-she-came-up-with-hogwarts-houses-on-the-back-of-airplane-vomit-bag-7607721

26. *List of best-selling books* https://en.wikipedia.org/wiki/List_of_best-selling_books

27. *The Ghost Club* https://en.wikipedia.org/wiki/The_Ghost_Club

28. *Of Mice and Men* https://en.wikipedia.org/wiki/Of_Mice_and_Men

29. *Shakespeare Day 2015: 10 facts you didn't know about William Shakespeare* https://www.coventrytelegraph.net/whats-on/whats-on-news/shakespeare-day-2015-10-facts-9091035

30. *To Kill a Mockingbird* https://en.wikipedia.org/wiki/To_Kill_a_Mockingbird

31. *Culture - The dark side of Roald Dahl* http://www.bbc.com/culture/story/20160912-the-dark-side-of-roald-dahl

32. *Pride and Prejudice* https://en.wikipedia.org/wiki/Pride_and_Prejudice

33. *Who is Silas Tomkyn Comberbache?* http://samueltaylorcoleridge.blogspot.com/2010/12/who-is-silas-tomkyn-comberbache.html

34. *Languages of Papua New Guinea* https://en.wikipedia.org/wiki/Languages_of_Papua_New_Guinea

35. *Does Bilingualism Delay the Onset of Dementia?* https://jeps.efpsa.org/articles/10.5334/jeps.375/

36. *Languages across Europe* http://www.bbc.co.uk/languages/european_languages/definitions.shtml

37. *The Languages of the World,* Kenneth Katzner

38. *Facts about the Lithuanian language* https://lithuaniatribune.com/facts-about-the-lithuanian-language/

39. *An Average American Knows 42,000 Words depending on how you count them* https://www.sciencemag.org/news/2016/08/average-20-year-old-american-knows-42000-words-depending-how-you-count-them

Sports & Leisure

Chess, rugby, LEGO, cooking or watching TV — whatever you're into, we all love taking part in some sort of leisure activity. Here are some amazing facts about sports & leisure.

The term pound cake originated from the pound of each of the four ingredients needed to make it.

• • •

As of July 2015, 600 billion LEGO parts have been created — that's 86 pieces for every person on Earth.

• • •

The silhouette on the NBA logo was modelled after Jerry West.

• • •

After the 2005 tsunami in Indonesia, Cristiano Ronaldo sponsored a 7-year-old boy who was spotted wearing a Portugal jersey. He went on to be signed by Lisbon in 2015.

The Cleveland Browns are the only team to neither play in or host a Super Bowl.

• • •

At the first modern Olympic games, winners were awarded silver medals, an olive branch and a diploma.

• • •

The most common number of dimples on a golf ball is 336.

• • •

Formula 1 drivers lose around 4 kgs of body weight and 3 litres of water after each race.

During the Super Bowl halftime, more toilets flush than at any other time of the year in the USA.

• • •

Belinda Clark was the first person to score a double century in a cricket ODI.

• • •

The last Olympic Games to give out medals made entirely of gold were in 1912.

• • •

The world's most wanted hacker was himself hacked and subsequently arrested because his password was his cat's name plus 123.

Three Olympic games have been held in countries that no longer exist.

• • •

The last time the Chicago Cubs won a World Series, the Ottoman Empire existed.

• • •

Adidas and Puma were founded by two brothers: Adolph and Rudolf Dassler. They were huge rivals.

• • •

Boxer Floyd Mayweather made $300 million in 2015 alone, which has made him the highest paid athlete in the world.

Only one in 3332 U.S. high school football players make it into the NFL.

• • •

The first toy to ever be advertised on television was Mr Potato Head, in 1952.

• • •

Liechtenstein has taken part in the most Olympic Games without winning any medals at all.

• • •

Shaquille O'Neal has a doctorate in education. He wrote his thesis on humor in the workplace.

Joe Gibbs is the only coach to have won the Super Bowl with three different quarterbacks.

• • •

Major League Baseball umpires are required to wear black underwear while on the job in case they split their pants.

• • •

A hardboiled egg will spin, whereas an uncooked or soft boiled egg will not.

• • •

Punters have the longest average NFL careers at 4.87 years.

The bushes in Super Mario Bros. were just recolored clouds.

• • •

The popular IOS game, Clash of Clans, makes an incredible 1.5 million dollars per day.

• • •

There are more possible iterations of chess than there are atoms in the entire universe.

• • •

It wasn't until 1907 that Major League Baseball teams started using numbers on their jerseys for identification.

Babe Ruth wore a cabbage leaf under his cap to keep him cool and he changed it over every two innings.

• • •

China didn't win an Olympic medal until 1984. However, at the 2004 Beijing Olympics, they won 100 medals.

• • •

The longest game of chess that is theoretically possible is has just over 5,000 moves.

The folding chess board was invented by a priest who was forbidden to play chess. The priest found a way around it by making a folding chess board. When folded together and put on a bookshelf, it simply looks like two books.

• • •

Track athletes are most likely to break records late in the day, when their body temperatures are highest.

• • •

The word "Checkmate" in Chess comes from the Persian phrase "Shah Mat," which means "the King is dead."

After his jerseys were stolen from the visitors locker room when the team was on the road against Orlando Magic, Jordan had to wear a No. 12 jersey.

• • •

Michael Jordan made $145 million in 2019, a large portion of which still comes from his shoe deal with Nike.

• • •

It takes 3,000 cows to supply the NFL with enough leather for a year's supply of footballs.

• • •

Alaska is the only state to have never sent a school to the NCAA Tournament.

The first chess board with alternating light and dark squares appeared in Europe in 1090.

• • •

Golf balls can reach speeds of over 170 miles an hour.

• • •

Pittsburgh is the only American city with three sports teams that wear the same colors.

• • •

Kareem Abdul-Jabbar, the NBA's all-time leading scorer (38,387 points), collects rugs.

Federer can be typed entirely with the left hand side of a keyboard.

• • •

While he was practicing baseball, Bulls and White Sox owner Jerry Reinsdorf was still paying Michael Jordan his $4 million annual basketball salary.

• • •

Four presidents have been on the cover of Sports Illustrated magazine: Bill Clinton, Ronald Reagan, John F. Kennedy and Gerald Ford.

The average lifespan of an MLB baseball is five to seven pitches.

• • •

Weight is more important for race car drivers than it is for runway models.

Sources

1. *Pound cake* https://en.wikipedia.org/wiki/Pound_cake

2. *Lego* https://en.wikipedia.org/wiki/Lego

3. *Does Jerry West Get Royalties For Being the NBA Logo?* https://www.mentalfloss.com/article/63937/does-jerry-west-get-royalties-being-nba-logo

4. *Martunis* https://en.wikipedia.org/wiki/Martunis

5. *List of Super Bowl champions* https://en.wikipedia.org/wiki/List_of_Super_Bowl_champions

6. *Athens 1896 Medals - Design, History & Photos* https://www.olympic.org/athens-1896-medals

7. *Q & A: How many dimples on a golf ball* https://van.physics.illinois.edu/qa/listing.php?id=947

8. *The human element – why the Singapore GP represents the biggest physical test of the season* https://motorsport.tech/formula-1/the-human-element-why-the-singapore-gp-represents-the-biggest-physical-test-of-the-season

9. *The Super Bowl of Toilets* https://www.thedailybeast.com/the-super-bowl-of-toilets

10. *Belinda Clark scored ODI cricket's first double hundred* https://inshorts.com/en/news/belinda-clark-scored-odi-crickets-first-double-hundred-1513408037520

11. *Gold medal* https://en.wikipedia.org/wiki/Gold_medal

12. *FBI's most wanted cyber criminal caught out by pet cat password* https://www.telegraph.co.uk/news/worldnews/northamerica/usa/11229241/FBIs-most-wanted-cyber-criminal-caught-out-by-pet-cat-password.html

13. *Past Countries at the Olympics* https://www.topendsports.com/events/summer/countries/countries-past.htm

14. *The Last Time The Cubs Won, The Ottoman Empire Still Existed* https://www.huffpost.com/entry/chicago-cubs-ottoman-empire-world-series_n_58179ce9e4b0390e69d1e30b

15. *Puma and Adidas' rivalry has divided a small German town for 70 years — here's what it looks like now* https://www.businessinsider.com/how-puma-and-adidas-rivalry-divided-their-founding-town-for-70-years-2018-10?IR=T

16. *Floyd Mayweather Net Worth 2020: Age, Height, Wife, Children, Bio, Wiki & Facts* https://www.raphaelsaadiq.com/biography-wiki-age-height-net-worth/boxer/floyd-mayweather-2019-2020-2021-2022/

17. *Getting Into the Game* https://operations.nfl.com/the-players/getting-into-the-game/

18. *Mr. Potato Head* https://en.wikipedia.org/wiki/Mr._Potato_Head

19. *Liechtenstein at the 2016 Summer Olympics* https://en.wikipedia.org/wiki/Liechtenstein_at_the_2016_Summer_Olympics

20. *Shaquille O'Neal Becomes Receives Doctorate Degree* https://abcnews.go.com/blogs/headlines/2012/05/shaquille-oneal-earns-ph-d-in-education

21. *Player BIO* https://www.profootballhof.com/players/joe-gibbs/biography/

22. *MLB Umpires Must Wear Black Underwear, In Case They Split Their Pants.* https://southfloridareporter.com/mlb-umpires-must-wear-black-underwear-in-case-they-split-their-pants/

23. *Article Title | Interact* http://www.physics.org/interact/physics-to-go/egg-citing-physics/index.html

24. *How Long Is the Average Career of an NFL Player?* https://careertrend.com/how-long-is-the-average-career-of-an-nfl-player-3032896.html

25. *The Clouds and Bushes in Super Mario Bros. are Identical* https://www.levelcodex.com/trivia/1-super-mario-cloud-bushes/

26. *Clash of Clans earns $1.5 million a day as top-grossing app* https://www.businessinsider.com/clash-of-clans-earns-15-million-a-day-as-top-grossing-app-2015-6?IR=T

27. *There Are More Games of Chess Possible Than Atoms In The Universe* https://curiosity.com/topics/there-are-more-games-of-chess-possible-than-atoms-in-the-universe-curiosity/

28. *Uniform number (Major League Baseball)* https://en.wikipedia.org/wiki/Uniform_number_(Major_League_Baseball)

29. *5 Quirky Facts About Babe Ruth* https://www.biography.com/news/babe-ruth-facts-biography

30. *China at the Olympics* https://en.wikipedia.org/wiki/China_at_the_Olympics

31. *The Longest Possible Chess Game* https://www.chess.com/blog/kurtgodden/the-longest-possible-chess-game

32. *Origins of Chess* https://www.chess.com/article/view/origins-of-chess

33. *100 Random Sports Facts You Never Knew* https://bleacherreport.com/articles/950303-100-random-sports-facts-you-never-knew

34. *Checkmate* https://en.wikipedia.org/wiki/Checkmate

35. *Michael Jordan once wore No. 12 with the Bulls* https://www.si.com/nba/2015/02/18/michael-jordan-bulls-jersey-number-12

36. *How Michael Jordan Will Make $145 Million In 2019* https://www.forbes.com/sites/kurtbadenhausen/2019/08/28/how-michael-jordan-will-make-145-million-in-2019/#544342761064

37. *Skin in the Game: From the Slaughterhouse to the Stadium* https://www.onegreenplanet.org/lifestyle/skin-in-the-game-from-the-slaughterhouse-to-the-stadium/

38. *Only one state has never had an NCAA tournament team* https://ftw.usatoday.

com/2014/03/ncaa-tournament-only-state-without-team-ever

39. *Origins of Chess* https://www.chess.com/article/view/origins-of-chess

40. *Swing Speed vs. Ball Speed* https://golftips.golfweek.com/swing-speed-vs-ball-speed-1637.html

41. *Sports in Pittsburgh* https://en.wikipedia.org/wiki/Sports_in_Pittsburgh

42. *Kareem Abdul-Jabbar selling rug collection at Minasian Rug Co. in Evanston* https://www.chicagobusiness.com/article/20160212/NEWS07/160219923/kareem-abdul-jabbar-selling-rug-collection-at-minasian-rug-co-in-evanston

43. *Hoop Dream* https://www.newsweek.com/hoop-dreams-180618

44. *Presidents on the Cover* https://www.si.com/more-sports/2008/11/04/04presidents-on-the-cover

45. *Fact of the Day: Average Life Span of a Major League Baseball* https://www.mlb.com/news/fact-of-the-day-average-life-span-of-a-major-league-baseball/c-35024016

Miscellaneous & Bizarre

We have thousands of facts up our sleeve... and some of them are just too bizarre to fit in another category — so here they are. Enjoy.

Boston has the highest number of berry-eaters in the United States.

• • •

More people die from selfies than shark attacks.

• • •

Around 65-81% percent of people can curl their tongue into a tube, with women more likely to be able to do it than men.

• • •

Millenials are estimated to return more than 75% of clothes they purchase online, while Baby Boomers return less than 50%.

The dot above the "i" is called a tittle.

• • •

"Vanity sizing" is the method some brands use to make customers feel slimmer than they are, by making clothes bigger than the label size suggests. Standard clothing sizes were scrapped in the US in 1983, so this is perfectly legal.

• • •

Diet soda has been shown to increase hunger.

• • •

You can find all the letters in the word 'typewriter' on one line of your keyboard.

A penny doubled every day becomes over five million dollars in just 30 days.

• • •

The number 2,520 can be divided by 1, 2, 3, 4, 5, 6, 7, 8, 9 and 10 without having a fractional leftover.

In the 1980's, Malaysia's King Mahmood Iskandah of Johor

• • •

The infinity sign is called a lemniscate.

• • •

Months that begin on a Sunday will always have a "Friday the 13th."

It is possible to turn a person's ashes into a diamond.

• • •

Over 95 percent of people who have lived to be over 110 are women.

• • •

There are more plastic flamingos in the USA than there are real ones.

• • •

The only 15 letter word that can be spelled without repeating a letter is "uncopyrightable".

14 squirrels were detained and charged with espionage on the Iranian border. They were allegedly carrying devices used to gather information.

• • •

If you are completely lost, head downhill — downhill leads to water, which eventually leads to people.

• • •

If you wear headphones in your ears for just one hour it will increase your ear's bacteria by 700 times.

• • •

Dead people can get goosebumps.

The longest official place name in the world is Taumatawhakatangihangakoauauotamateapokai-whenuakitanatahu, a hill in New Zealand.

• • •

If you find a lost driver's license in the USA you can just drop it into a mailbox and the postman will deliver it back to its owner.

• • •

To stay healthy you only technically have to have a shower once or twice a week. We do so more regularly for vanity reasons.

• • •

It is estimated that upto 1 billion birds die every year from smashing into windows.

A surfer once sued another surfer for 'stealing his wave'.

• • •

The Statue of Liberty wears a size 879 sandal.

• • •

Hurricanes with women's names kill more people than those with men's.

• • •

The face of a penny can hold approximately 30 drops of water.

No piece of paper can be folded in half more than 12 times.

• • •

In a set of 23 randomly chosen people, there is a 50 percent probability of two people having the same birthday.

• • •

Nearly half of all U.S. college students drop out before they get a degree.

• • •

The Maruyama Zoo in Japan spent four years trying to get two hyenas to mate before realising they were both male.

It takes approximately 66 days for a habit to stick.

• • •

Pogonophobia is the fear of beards.

• • •

People who regularly take naps tend to die younger than those who don't.

• • •

If you are a redhead you might be able to get a high school scholarship that is only for redheads!

• • •

In French, the word 'avocat' means both avocado and lawyer.

An American artist by the name of Pope.L has eaten entire issues of the Wall Street Journal and belly-crawled around the entirety of Manhattan. He refers to himself as a 'fisherman of social absurdity'.

• • •

Despite popular belief, urine does not cure jellyfish stings. It can actually make them worse.

• • •

Around a third of all murders in the USA go unsolved.

• • •

Before Harry Houdini died, he left very detailed information about how he would contact his loved ones after his death.

McDonald's created the McRib in 1981 after the introduction of Chicken Nuggets were so popular they resulted in a chicken shortage.

• • •

There is a blind guy who can ride his bike in traffic using echolocation.

• • •

The fashion designer Karl Lagerfield had 300 iPods. He hired someone whose sole job was to take care of them.

• • •

It was illegal to sell sex toys in Texas until 2008. It is still illegal in Alabama.

Seventy-four percent of American couples who were married in 2018 created a wedding website.

• • •

In 2012 in Sweden a man named Peter Skyllberg managed to stay alive in his snowed-in car for two months by staying warm in his sleeping bag and eating snow.

• • •

There is a website that allows you to anonymously send animal poop to a person.

Sources

1. *More People Died From Selfies Than Shark Attacks This Year, Report Says* https://www.health.com/pain/selfie-shark-attack-deaths-mashable

2. *Driscoll's Unveils the Top 10 Berry-Loving Markets in America* https://www.businesswire.com/news/home/20170629005313/en/Driscoll%E2%80%99s-Unveils-Top-10-Berry-Loving-Markets-America

3. *Myths of Human Genetics: Tongue Rolling* https://udel.edu/~mcdonald/myth-tongueroll.html

4. *Ecommerce Trends in 2020 (+147 Statistics About Online Shopping)* https://www.bigcommerce.com/blog/ecommerce-trends/

5. *Tittle* https://en.wikipedia.org/wiki/Tittle

6. *Vanity sizing* https://en.wikipedia.org/wiki/Vanity_sizing

7. *member: Pope.L, 1978–2001* https://www.moma.org/calendar/exhibitions/5059

8. *Here's the Science That Explains Why Drinking Diet Soda Makes You Gain Weight* https://www.inc.com/minda-zetlin/diet-soda-weight-gain-metabolism-insulin-brain-fat-metabolic-syndrome.html

9. *Double a Penny Every Day for 30 Days... Now Pay Taxes* https://nomadcapitalist.com/2019/05/03/double-a-penny/

10. *SOLUTION: what is the lowest number possible that when divided by 1, 2, 3, 4, 5, 6, 7, 8, 9, and 10 always has one left over, or a remainder of one? thanks a bunch.* https://www.algebra.com/algebra/homework/word/numbers/Numbers_Word_Problems.faq.question.223183.html

11. *Houdini's Promise to Prove Life After Death* https://exemplore.com/paranormal/Houdinis-Promise

12. *Infinity symbol* https://en.wikipedia.org/wiki/Infinity_symbol

13. *Is true that if the first of the month begins on a Sunday, the month will always have a Friday the 13th?* https://www.quora.com/Is-true-that-if-the-first-of-the-month-begins-on-a-Sunday-the-month-will-always-have-a-Friday-the-13th

14. *Can a person's ashes be turned into a diamond?* https://www.heart-in-diamond.com/can-turn-person-ashes-diamonds.html

15. *Why are 95% of people who live to 110 women? You're as old as your stem cells* https://www.sciencedaily.com/releases/2015/06/150604141903.htm

16. *Facts That Sounds Like They Are Not True - Crazy Trivia - What Was The First Thing Ever Bought On The Internet* https://www.thrillist.com/culture/facts-that-sounds-like-they-are-not-true-crazy-trivia-what-was-the-first-thing-ever-bought-on-the-internet

17. *McRib* https://en.wikipedia.org/wiki/McRib

18. *Karl Lagerfeld Dies With A Beautiful, Flawed Legacy* https://www.refinery29.com/en-us/2019/02/224870/karl-lagerfeld-fashion-designer-legacy

19. *Word Trivia* - https://stevelaube.com/fun-fridays-word-trivia/

20. *Iranians arrest 14 squirrels for spying* https://www.ynetnews.com/articles/0,7340,L-3425130,00.html

21. *How to find your way out of the woods without tools—or your phone* https://www.popsci.com/navigate-without-tools-or-phone/

22. *Get poo delivered to your enemy's door just in time for Christmas* https://www.mirror.co.uk/news/weird-news/poo-delivered-your-enemys-door-4562728

23. *Wearing Headphones For Just An Hour Can Increase Bacteria In Ears By 700 Times* https://theproenzablog.com/featured/wearing-headphones-for-just-an-hour-can-increase-bacteria-in-ears-by-700-times/

24. *8 Myths About Dead Bodies You Probably Think Are True* https://www.mentalfloss.com/article/514257/8-myths-about-dead-bodies-you-probably-think-are-true

25. *Taumatawhakatangihangakoauauotamateaturipukakapikimaungahoronuku-pokaiwhenuakitanatahu* https://en.wikipedia.org/wiki/Taumatawhakatangihangakoau-auotamateaturipukakapikimaungahoronukupokaiwhenuakitanatahu

26. *Return a Lost Driver's License By Dropping It In Any Mailbox* https://lifehacker.com/return-a-lost-drivers-license-by-dropping-it-in-any-ma-510418965

27. *Showering daily — is it necessary? - Harvard Health Blog* https://www.health.harvard.edu/blog/showering-daily-is-it-necessary-2019062617193

28. *How many birds are killed by windows?* https://www.bbc.com/news/magazine-22395664

29. *Here are a few of surfing's most high-profile lawsuits* https://www.mensjournal.com/adventure/here-are-a-few-of-surfings-most-high-profile-lawsuits/

30. *20 Statue of Liberty Facts | HowStuffWorks* https://adventure.howstuffworks.com/20-facts-about-the-statue-of-liberty.htm

31. *Female hurricanes are deadlier than male hurricanes* https://www.pnas.org/content/111/24/8782

32. *Measure Surface Tension with a Penny* https://www.scientificamerican.com/article/measure-surface-tension-with-a-penny/

33. *WATCH: What Happens When You Try to Fold Paper More Than 7 Times With a Hydraulic Press?* https://www.sciencealert.com/watch-what-happens-when-you-try-to-fold-paper-more-than-7-times-with-a-hydraulic-press

34. *Birthday problem* https://en.wikipedia.org/wiki/Birthday_problem

35. *The Cost of College Dropout* https://www.thebalance.com/the-cost-of-college-dropout-4174303

36. *Zoo realises it has been trying to mate two male hyenas for four years* https://www.itv.com/news/2014-10-03/zoo-realises-it-has-been-trying-to-mate-two-male-hyenas-for-four-years/

37. *Here's How Long It Really Takes to Break a Habit, According to Science* https://www.sciencealert.com/how-long-it-takes-to-break-a-habit-according-to-science

38. *Pogonophobia* https://en.wikipedia.org/wiki/Pogonophobia

39. *Mid-Day Naps Can Be a Sign of Bad Health* https://www.smithsonianmag.com/smart-news/consistently-needing-take-long-mid-day-naps-might-be-indicative-underlying-health-problem-180951071/

40. *Scholarships for Redhead 2020-2021 | USA Scholarships* https://worldscholarship-forum.com/redhead-scholarship/

41. *The Difference between Avocado and Lawyer in French* https://www.livinglanguage.com/blog/2012/01/19/the-difference-between-avocado-and-lawyer-in-french/

42. *Fact or Fiction?: Urinating on a Jellyfish Sting is an Effective Treatment* https://www.scientificamerican.com/article/fact-or-fiction-urinating/

43. *Open Cases: Why One-Third Of Murders In America Go Unresolved* https://www.npr.org/2015/03/30/395069137/open-cases-why-one-third-of-murders-in-america-go-unresolved

44. *Texas obscenity statute* https://en.wikipedia.org/wiki/Texas_obscenity_statute

45. *Wedding trends that did not exist before the 2010s* https://www.insider.com/wedding-trends-that-did-not-exist-before-the-2010s-2019-12

46. *A Californian Blind Man Uses Echolocation To Ride A Bike* https://inhabitat.com/california-blind-man-uses-echolocation-to-navigate-around-on-his-bike/

47. *Swedish man survived for two months in snowbound car thanks to 'igloo' effect* https://www.telegraph.co.uk/news/worldnews/europe/sweden/9091674/Swedish-man-survived-for-two-months-in-snowbound-car-thanks-to-igloo-effect.html

And that's all, folks! I hope you enjoyed these facts and learned some interesting things to share with your family and friends.

I would very much appreciate your review on Amazon — it helps me to make bigger and better books next time!

If you'd like more facts books, search 'Jenny Kellett' on Amazon to find my author page.

Printed by Amazon Italia Logistica S.r.l.
Torrazza Piemonte (TO), Italy

16198191R00141